The Depression Pilgrim's Journey

The Man Who Walked through Time

Paul A. Ritch

Copyright © 2025 by Paul A. Ritch

All rights reserved.

No part of this book may be reproduced, stored in a retrieval system, or transmitted in any form or by any means—electronic, mechanical, photocopying, recording, or otherwise—without the prior written permission of the publisher, except for brief quotations used in reviews or scholarly works.

Table of Contents

Acknowledgements _____ 2
Dedication to Joyce _____ 5
Introduction _____ 8
Chapter 1 The Formative Years _____ 10
    But you can get there from here! _____ 10
    The Luxury of Poverty _____ 11
Chapter 2 The Defining Years _____ 15
    From Adolescence to Adulthood in a Single Day _____ 15
    The "Not Cotton" Business _____ 19
    Teenage High School Algebra Teacher _____ 22
    Teenage School Bus Driver _____ 24
    The Rock Altar - 1953 _____ 28
Chapter 3 The Later Years _____ 31
    No Regrets _____ 31
    Pastor, Evangelist, Educator, Counselor, and Computer Pioneer: _____ 34
    An Exit Ramp to a Roadside Revival _____ 42
    A Working Evangelist _____ 51
    Car in my reserved parking space _____ 54
    Paul and CSTI IBM 1620 1967 _____ 56
    Additional Memory Salesman 1969 _____ 57
    Additional Memory Manager 1969 _____ 58
    Paul Content Winner Seymour Freely 1970 _____ 60
    Paul Seymour Freely Winner 1970 _____ 61
    Paul National Contest Winner Seymour Freely 1970 _____ 62
    Paul Presenting CSTI Graduate Degrees _____ 63
    Trena First Enrollee CSTI Secretarial Science _____ 64
    Paul Articulating Rep to SUCCST 1975 _____ 65
    PAR with the co-developer of the world's 1st computer ____ 66
    Paul with Dr. Prespert Exckert _____ 67
    Paul Certified Manager 1980 _____ 68

Joyce's Surprise 60th Birthday Party 09/21/1991	70
Paul and Joyce Plains, GA 1998	71
Paul A. Ritch 2006	72
Paul A. Ritch 2010	73
CSTCC Data Center Dedication (1) 2018	74
CSTCC Data Center Dedication (2) 2018	75
Paul Honor CSTCC 2018	77
Paul DD214 Destroyed in Fire 2022	79
Chapter 4 The Golden Years	82
The Providential Purpose and Plan in Pain	82
(Versus, how we deal with it)	82
In Loving Memory of Joyce Ann Price Ritch	88
09/22/1931 – 07/15/2017	88
Safe in the New Year	91
Chapter 5 Collections of Humor	93
Communication Albert Mehrabian	93
Often confusing English words	94
Communication Problem	95
Halleys Breakdown in Communication	97
Pilot who Speaks Blonde	98
If, when you say "Whiskey" (Courtesy, Paul A. Ritch)	100
Grandmother Witness	102
49 Actual Newspaper Headlines (collected by journalists)	104
Church Bulletin Bloopers	107
'SIGNS' of the Times	109
Excerpts from the Hospital	111
A Few of Life's Little 'Mysteries'	113
Holy Humor	116
Humor Stupidity	117
Perspective	120
The Barometer Story	122
Don't Let Go of the Rope!	126

If Jesus Came Today	129
Paul's Occupation List	131
Paulisms (2025)	133
Paul's Tests Administered During His Career	138
Square Test of Logic	140
Wrong Thing to Say	141
Chapter 6 Closing Thoughts	143
Why I Believe the Bible to be the Word of God	143
God's Wonders and Miracles	148
The Amazing Camel and its Creator	150
Reality of the Unseen	164
Shipwreck Survivor	167
Greek Time Kairos vs Chronos	168
Proof of the Human Soul	169
The Soul's Weight (1983)	170
The Laminins Cross in our Bodies	171
Israel's Order of the Camps	175
Noah's Ark Lessons	176
Cohn's Law	177
Murphy's Fundamental Laws	178
Murphy's Addends, or 'The Gospel according to Ritch'	179
Born Before 1945	181
Excuses vs. Commitment II Timothy 2:2; II Timothy 4:1-ff	184
Appendix A: About the Author	192
Paul A. Ritch Education, Experience, Honors, Etc.	192
Paul A. Ritch Representative Clients	201
Appendix B: Poems	206
Then	206
A Tree	207
I Met God	210
I've Dreamed Many Dreams	211
A Builder	213

At My Mother's Knee	215
I Miss You	217
If	218
Appendix C: Selected works of Art by Joyce	220
What Will Matter	225
Paul Ritch link to YouTube:	227

The Depression Pilgrim's Journey
The Man Who Walked through Time

The Depression Pilgrim's Journey
The Man Who Walked through Time

Acknowledgements

To my precious deceased wife, **Joyce Ann,** who labored with me in this long journey; who helped absorb the vexation of countless tribulations; who encouraged me through many reverses; whose companionship afforded my life a DEEP sense of fulfillment; who encouraged me to compile a memory booklet of my life experiences; I owe a great debt and to whom I especially give my love and eternal devotion.

To the children Barbara, Sherman, Trena, Gary, David, and Dennis, who were denied time with me during the long months of sustained study, preparation, and evangelistic travels.

And, to our daughter, **Trena Ann Holladay,** my long-time assistant, I owe a deep debt.

I owe special thanks to the **Rev. Harvey Brown**, my Pastor, my mentor, my role model, and my friend. It was Harvey who led me to the Lord, nurtured me, taught me, licensed me, under whom I served an internship, and who later presided over my ordination. He provided me with materials from author Paul Holdcraft, Zondervan Publications, and others, all of which helped me enormously in study habits and springboard to platform preparation for Christian and secular audiences sprinkled with humor.

The Depression Pilgrim's Journey
The Man Who Walked through Time

I owe a deep debt of gratitude to **Henry Brown** (Harvey Brown's brother), who was my Sunday School teacher, my mentor, my one-time employer, and my special friend.

Special thanks to the **Rev. Hosea Mull,** who mentored me, guided me, encouraged me, and shared his pulpit with me.

And, to **Ben Haden**, my Pastor for more than thirty years at 1st Presbyterian Church Chattanooga (FPCC); my confidant; my treasured and dearest friend; and, with whom I worked in his "Changed Lives" Radio-TV-Internet ministry from its beginning in 1967 until his home going (10-24-2013), I owe eternal gratitude.

Many thanks to the resources of **Rev. Clarence Larkin,** a prolific writer; **Rev. C. I. Scofield** for his invaluable commentaries; **Fred H. Wight; Dr. Mark Cambron; and Tennessee Temple Bible School and College;** Trinity Bible Seminary; the University of Tennessee at Chattanooga; the University of Tennessee at Knoxville; The Gideons; Billy Sunday; Bible Soft; Charles Spurgeon; Matthew Henry; Adam Clarke; Barnes Notes; and myriad others.

I have no claim of originality.

May God add his blessings to this effort. It is NOT about me; it has NEVER been about me; it is about Him! John the Baptist got it right. John said, "He (Jesus) must increase, I must decrease"

The Depression Pilgrim's Journey
The Man Who Walked through Time

(John 3:30)! To that end, may these observations from many decades spark an interest in the reader. To the only wise God our Savior, be glory, majesty, dominion, and power both now and ever! Amen (Jude 25).

Paul A. Ritch

The Depression Pilgrim's Journey
The Man Who Walked through Time

Dedication to Joyce

Joyce Ann Ritch: putting God first; husband and children next; then others; And, finally, herself last; became a living legend with far-reaching, pervasive impact.

A native of Bradley County, Tennessee, Joyce attended the public schools of McMinn County, TN, and then lived her late teens and all of her adult life in the Chattanooga area. Devoted to her Savior, to her husband Paul, and the children: Barbara (Deceased 05-09-2019), Sherman (Wanda), Trena (Tim), Gary, David (Deceased 08-05-2015), Dennis, and several grandchildren and great-grandchildren.

An aesthetician, wife, mother, and homemaker without equal, after retiring in 1973, she studied Art at Chattanooga State for one year and UT Chattanooga for eight years to enhance her already unmatched gift. She was an accomplished artist, but early life tragedies left her with low self-esteem. So, I named her still life paintings and exhibited her mixed-media non-objective representational works of art in many regional locations, where she won numerous regional juried competitions, including 1st place at the High Museum in Atlanta, Georgia, the pinnacle of the art world.

Her paintings have hung in many private collections throughout the region, and individual works have hung in numerous corporate offices (public and private), including Standard Oil of Ohio, SCR

The Depression Pilgrim's Journey
The Man Who Walked through Time

Corporation, Management Improvement Services, Ritch-King Enterprises, and government offices including GSA, US Treasury, TVA, NASA, and numerous legal and medical facilities in the southeastern U. S. Although she has been wife and mother par excellence, her most crowning attribute was her steadfast love and devotion to her Lord and Savior, Jesus Christ. She quietly witnessed for Him, and people were drawn to her because of her genuineness and love for Him. Children gravitated to her, and she was known as 'Mom' to scores of those little urchins whom she impacted. She was a lifetime member of the Gideons International Auxiliary and a long-time active member and Sunday School teacher at Mt. Olive Baptist Church in north Georgia. Then, an active member for decades at 1st Presbyterian Church of Chattanooga (FPCC) and its "ladies in the Church," where she was affectionately known as the 'apple pie lady' for the hundreds to whom she so ministered in hospitals, nursing homes, convalescent centers, homebound, neighbors, and countless others, just because.

In her final years she was devastated by two left body strokes; simultaneous alternating Hashimoto's and Graves' Diseases; necessitating total annihilation of the thyroid gland (the great 'regulator'); end-stage Parkinson's; life threatening COPD & asthma (five breathing treatments daily); crippling neuropathy in both legs; Shy-Dragger Syndrome; immune system completely compromised putting her at great risk; almost totally deaf; early macular degeneration and gradual loss of vision from Parkinson's damage to retina nerves; debilitating gastroparesis; challenging memory issues from cerebral concussion and Alzheimer's; vasovagal syncope with periodic heart stoppage (clinically dead five times); severe allergy to sulfa and red dye; and catastrophic pulmonary aspiration destroying the epiglottis in late June 2017. No longer able to swallow except pureed and sitting upright, under Hospice Crisis Care with husband Paul holding her hand, Joyce escaped this prison of clay and "Beat him home" to be with the Lord in the early morning hours of July 15, 2017.

Joyce embodied all that God intended a woman to be as a wife, mother, homemaker, prayer partner, best friend, and dedicated Christian! This effort is lovingly dedicated to her as a token of my eternal love and deep appreciation for more than half a century of mutually devoted companionship and friendship.

Dr. Paul A. Ritch, eternally grateful and mutually devoted spouse

The Depression Pilgrim's Journey
The Man Who Walked through Time

Introduction

I was born an original during the Great Depression with two universal innate drives:

    1) a sucking reflex action that sustained life by nursing; and,

    2) a fear of falling.

Everything else I 'learned', I soon became an admixture "copy" of all that I encountered. I have no claim of originality. Everything I know I learned from some source or someone. I gleaned, I learned, I meditated, I benefited from, and I "En-Ritched" where it seemed appropriate.

I became a teacher early on when the credentialing process was in its rather formative stage. A large part of my life I taught at many levels: High School, Colleges, and Universities (Private, Public, and Parochial Doctoral and post-Doctoral levels). As a teacher, I learned early that, to get audience attention, it helped if one could make them laugh. Later, I share "Paulisms."

I tried to develop a strategy of a different way of saying the same thing as others would say, but in different words. In that process, my students at all levels began to share with me items of unique expressions and humor. Over the ensuing years, I collected hundreds of such items. This collection of autobiographical

The Depression Pilgrim's Journey
The Man Who Walked through Time

remembrances, recollections, and humor comes from my own experiences and includes those given to me by others.

I am indebted to all who contributed to this collection. I have given credit where I recalled. If I have neglected or overlooked any credit, it is an error of the head and not of the heart. Please disregard any flaws, errors, or omissions the reader may discover, and accept this as an attempt from hundreds collected over several decades to share a meaningful number of those.

And God said, "Let there be Light" (Gen. 1:1).

And Paul said, "Let there be humor".

Paul A. Ritch

Chapter 1
The Formative Years
But you can get there from here!

The story of one man's plight from abject poverty to the peaks of Providential pardon, peace, provision, protection, power, and preservation, and a pending home promised by the Supreme Architect!

When you have reached the end of all that you know, and it's time for a leap of faith, you can take that leap of faith in full assurance that God is going to do either one of two things:

1. He's either going to prepare you a safe place to land,

2. Or …. He's going to teach you how to fly!

Portions borrowed and "En-Ritched" by Paul A. Ritch

There always seemed to be a prevailing providential plan and purpose for the painful, pressing, and perplexing problems that presented themselves to the pilgrim of the deep depression era.

The Depression Pilgrim's Journey
The Man Who Walked through Time

The Luxury of Poverty

I was born into abject poverty in rural northwest Georgia during the great depression. My Dad was mostly missing, choosing to neglect his family and chase everything that wore a skirt, and finally left us altogether. My mom was severely impaired (and died years later from medical neglect). I had one brother and one sister. In those days, there were no outreach programs from the government or local Churches. There were no paved roads (even U.S. Highway 27 was not paved in some places), no electricity, no running water, and very little food. It quickly fell upon me to become the "man of the house".

I went to a nearby saw mill and retrieved pine bark "slabs" (discarded bark and minimum wood trimmed from the log prior to sawing precut timbers). From these scraps, I made crude rabbit traps and placed them in strategic places for maximum trapping potential. I traded the rabbits I caught to a rural rolling store for flour, corn meal, and essentials from which I could make bread for the family.

But for the kindness of a relative who donated an old mule and an abandoned plough with which I could make a garden to grow vegetables (food for summer and canned for winter), we would have starved.

The Depression Pilgrim's Journey
The Man Who Walked through Time

Times were hard. Winters were harsh, and the only heat was from a donated small laundry heater, fired with small timbers cut from nearby woods. Medical help was unavailable. I never had shoes bought for me until I was in the third grade. I picked cotton in nearby farms, bought for the family first, and when there was sufficient left, I bought a pair of cheap shoes for myself of the type largely worn by the poorest. Prior to that, I rummaged and found discarded shoes with large holes in the soles. I traced the outline on cardboard, cut it out, and placed the cardboard inside to keep my feet from being on the ground through the holes in the discarded shoes. This way of life continued until I was in my early teens. I will address this later in an article I chose to call "From Adolescence to Adulthood in a single day".

Why do I say "The Luxury of Poverty"? Because the poverty and hardship taught values that one cannot buy with money and that are worth MORE than money! It prepared me for life where one does not always get their desires and has to be disciplined and regimented. It conditioned me to want something and have to wait, as opposed to the contemporary mindset, like unto the five-hundred-pound parrot who said, "I want my cracker NOW!" This experience taught me not to go into debt except for large purchases like a car or a house. This is a "luxury". I internalized those values from the poverty that I endured and survived.

The Depression Pilgrim's Journey
The Man Who Walked through Time

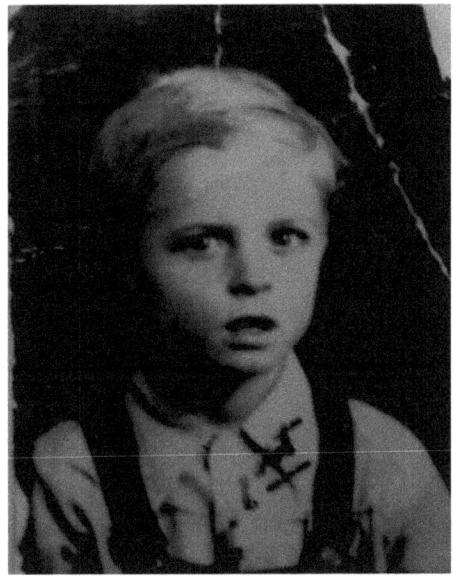

Paul's 1st Grade

Paul's 3rd Grade

Paul's 6th Grade

Paul's 11th Grade

The Depression Pilgrim's Journey
The Man Who Walked through Time

End of Chapter

Chapter 2
The Defining Years
From Adolescence to Adulthood in a Single Day

The year was 1951. The place was the Cedartown, Georgia Commercial National Bank. The individuals were Bank President Mr. W. D. Tripp, my Uncle R. T. Ritch, my brother Larry, and this writer. My brother was impaired from a catastrophic fall as a toddler into an open fireplace, damaging the frontal lobe. Therefore, I became by default the head of the house.

I mentioned in an earlier writing that we were left destitute and in abject poverty, and that a gracious neighbor had given us a mule and a discarded plough with which I could till the ground and raise vegetables for meager food, and then can some for the harsh winter months. Whether it was accidental or on cruel purpose, I shall never know, but someone killed our mule. We were thus left totally destitute and with no foreseeable means of survival. There were no government or local Church outreach programs in those depression days. Times were harsh.

I became a Christian as a 13-year-old teenager. I began sharing my faith in the classroom, on the streets, in the jails, in cottage prayer services, and in local churches at their request. I became a teenage speaker on a local radio station (WGAA-1340) and a local TV station (WROM-TV, now Chattanooga WTVC-TV9), both sponsored by others, and soon became a regular teenage speaker across the region. Thus, I was somewhat known by name for those who had tuned in and listened.

One of my Dad's brothers was an officer in the U. S. Army Air Force, as it was then called, before becoming a separate branch of the military. As God would have it, Uncle R.T. came home on leave just after this tragedy had occurred. As we tearfully told him of our plight, he said that he had an idea. He told my brother and me to get ready, and we went into the nearby town to a local bank. He described to the bank president our plight and said to him as follows, "I am these youngsters' uncle. I know their character. They will honor their word as sacred, and Paul is a very dedicated and devout Christian and would never go back on his word. Someone killed their mule (their only chance of survival), and I am asking you to give these youngsters a loan with which to buy a small tractor. I will not co-sign a loan note, but I give you my word as a United States military officer that, if they do not repay you, I will."

As my brother and I sat across from the massive desk of the bank president, Mr. W.D. Tripp, said to us, "Boys, if I loan you this money, you will need to sign a promissory note that you will repay it. The promissory note will be worthless to me because you are minors, and I could never collect it. I would have to repay it myself because I alone am responsible for this bank's resources, but it will

The Depression Pilgrim's Journey
The Man Who Walked through Time

be to you a constant reminder of your sacred obligation. Will you reach over my desk, shake my hand, look me in the eye, and give me your sacred word that you will repay me?"

I arose, reached over the massive desk, shook his hand, and said to Mr. Tripp, "I give you my sacred word as a Christian that I will repay you if you give us a loan." My brother did likewise.

Mr. Tripp said, "Go down the street to the tractor dealership, find the most reasonable one that will meet your needs, come back to me, and we will talk."

We did and came back to the bank and advised him. He had already drawn up the papers requiring only the loan amount. My brother and I both signed the promissory note. My uncle R. T. did not sign it. Mr. Tripp then sat down, wrote out a check for $1,310, with which we purchased a small Farmall Cub tractor. It is a rare likelihood that a teenager with no assets and nothing to provide as security but his word would be trusted and given a loan secured only by his handshake and oath. That is extremely rare and a throwback to a much simpler time. One cannot enforce a contract from someone who has not yet reached the age of majority.

Word spread in that small town, and I was able as a teenager to open lines of credit upon my word that I would raise "money crops" and repay in the fall harvest. I opened lines of credit in the

The Depression Pilgrim's Journey
The Man Who Walked through Time

feed and supply stores and the gas merchant who delivered and filled a tank with gas for the tractor (gas for farm use was 11 cents a gallon). I may be one of only a very few teenagers in history to have open lines of credit based only upon a promise that I would repay.

It took three years, but I was able to repay the bank and all other loans in full while still a teenager. I went into that bank that memorable day as a teenager, and, due to the trust placed in me, I came out as a man!

God is SO good!

The Depression Pilgrim's Journey
The Man Who Walked through Time

The "Not Cotton" Business

Now in possession of farming equipment (the aforementioned Farmall Cub tractor), I was able to plant cash crops (primarily, cotton) and harvest enough to pay my indebtedness and sufficient left over to buy things for the family.

It brought me great joy to buy for my mom and my younger sister, whom I reared more like a father figure than a brother. But, alas, the medical help came too late for my mom.

The issues had taken their toll, and she died as a young woman in her forties. Fifty dollars of necessary medical intervention would have saved her. My main cash crop was cotton, but it was expensive to grow, and the profit at harvest time was not enormous.

The cost of seed and fertilizer was a factor, but the greater expense was treating for boll weevils, which I had to hire done because that equipment was too expensive to own.

The labor-intensive part of hoeing out the weeds on the rows I did myself in long and hard days. Plowing the weeds out in the middle between the rows was easy. I could ride and do that!

In grades nine and ten, while others signed up for "Study Hall", I signed up for a class called "Vocational Agriculture". Mr. Trimble was the teacher's name. Because Study Hall would be a piece of cake, just goofing off, a few of us had decided to go for

The Depression Pilgrim's Journey
The Man Who Walked through Time

some information that would benefit us. Because of the small enrollment and the total devotion of this Godly man, I was able to glean pointers from him on how to maximize profits from farming.

Mr. Trimble took a special liking to me, visited me in the remote country, and gave me some lucrative pointers. He had me parallel test the costs and resulting profit between raising my best acre in cotton and my worst acre in pimento peppers.

There was no natural enemy to pimento peppers, so the profit difference was dramatic! I then began raising only pimento peppers. I got out of the "cotton business".

In their supposed wisdom, the U. S. Government had built massive warehouses and bought up the cotton to keep it off the market and maintain "parity". So, I never sold a bale of cotton to private industry. The government bought it. When that plan fizzled, the U. S. Government started paying farmers NOT to grow cotton.

The County Agent visited me and said the government would pay me not to grow cotton. I said, "I am no longer growing cotton. I grow only pimento peppers." So, I am not a candidate. He, abiding by governmental guidelines, began paying me to not grow cotton.

So, I was now in the "Not Cotton" business!

The Depression Pilgrim's Journey
The Man Who Walked through Time

Who's Who

Cedartown (GA) High School

Most Intellectual
PAUL RITCH   PEGGY LANIER

The Depression Pilgrim's Journey
The Man Who Walked through Time

Teenage High School Algebra Teacher

The year was 1953. The place was Cedartown (Polk County), Georgia. The subjects were Mr. W. B. Thomas, High School Principal; first-year algebra students; and this writer.

A brief backdrop will set the stage for how I became a High School teacher. It is a novel sequence of events as to how I became a high school teacher while still a senior in high school myself. At that time, the school teacher credentialing process was rather in the primitive/formative stage. When I was young, a person could teach a subject so long as they had taken and passed the course. As a High School senior (17 years old), I had taken and passed first-year algebra, second-year algebra, geometry, and trigonometry.

In those days, as you went to each class on the first day of school, the teacher would hand out an assignment sheet on purple "ditto" paper (This was before the advent of modern copiers), which listed the text book for the course, the assignment dates for reading and preparation for each class meeting, the homework assignments along with the date each test would be given. I was born into abject poverty in remote rural northwest Georgia and grew up hard. My dad had neglected and essentially abandoned us.

My mom was severely impaired, in need of life-saving medical intervention, later became totally disabled, and eventually died from medical neglect. I did not have the luxury of idle time. So,

The Depression Pilgrim's Journey
The Man Who Walked through Time

while others were essentially playing during "study hall", I read all the assigned materials, worked all the homework assignments, turned them in in advance, never took any books home with me, and just showed up to take the tests. I was always finished by Thanksgiving and only attended class after that to take the tests. Problem. You had to attend a certain number of days in order to qualify for grades.

Problem. I was the valedictorian. Are you going to fail the valedictorian? Unlikely. What to do? What to do? Solution. Mr. W. B. Thomas, principal, a Godly man, called for me to come to his office. He assigned me to teach first-year algebra in order to get me on campus to count as a day of "attendance." This is the same Mr. Thomas who later "drafted" me to drive a 60-passenger school bus filled with giggling High School girls and two female teachers to North Georgia College in Dahlonega, Georgia, for a State meeting. But that's a story for another time.

I taught first-year algebra to the freshmen students while still a senior student myself. I still have my senior yearbook in which my students wrote kind and gracious words as to how I had impacted their lives, not only as a teacher, but as a provider of direction, arming them as "living messages" which I was sending to the future. God is SO good!

The Depression Pilgrim's Journey
The Man Who Walked through Time

Teenage School Bus Driver

The year was 1953. The place was Cedartown (Polk County), Georgia. The subjects were Mr. W. B. Thomas, High School Principal; a gaggle of giggling High School girls; two unmarried female High School teachers; a conscripted male student; and this writer.

In an earlier document, I recounted how I became an unlikely teenage High School algebra teacher. Here, I will recount how that same cagey High School principal, Mr. W. B. Thomas, "drafted" me as a 17-year-old senior to drive a 60-passenger school bus filled with giggling High School girls and two female High School teachers to a State conference at North Georgia College in the mountains of Dahlonega, Georgia.

Mr. Thomas sent for me to come to his office, and I went as he had requested. When I entered his office, he said, "Paul, you can drive a bus, can't you?"

I replied, "No, I've never driven a bus. I've only driven a car, a tractor, and my uncle's pickup truck".

He said, "I think you can drive a bus. It just has more gears." As if he had driven a bus!

The Depression Pilgrim's Journey
The Man Who Walked through Time

I replied, "That may be accurate, but I am not authorized to drive a passenger vehicle. It is my understanding that I would have to have a chauffeur's license."

I thought that would take care of the matter at hand and that would be the end of it. But I might have suspected that would not be the end. It wasn't. In keeping with his crafty way of finding a solution to a complex situation, he said, "I think I can take care of that. You see, I know the local Georgia Highway Patrol Colonel in charge; we are in the same Sunday School class".

With that said, he picked up the phone and placed a call.

In the quiet office, I could hear both parties to the call. When the phone was answered, Mr. Thomas said to the Colonel, "I have a pressing issue, and I think you might be able to help me. You see, I had arranged for a driver to take a bus full of girls and two teachers to a State Conference in North Georgia, and the driver had emergency surgery, and I need an alternate driver. I have a young man here that I think can do that for me, but he feels that to do that legally, he would need a chauffeur's license".

The Colonel said, "What's the young man's name, date of birth, and mailing address?"

Mr. Thomas gave him all the information, and the Colonel said for Mr. Thomas to have me stop by the Patrol office after school

The Depression Pilgrim's Journey
The Man Who Walked through Time

and ask for him personally, and he would talk with me. I went by that afternoon, and he gave me a Chauffeur's license!

The scariest thing I ever did in my entire life was to drive that loaded 60-passenger school bus through a winding highway to Dahlonega, Georgia.... not the later military service hugging the ground, crawling under a wall of live-fire tracer bullets 18" above your head training for possible deployment to a war zone; not being shot at and missed ... but driving that school bus filled with passengers up a dangerous serpentine mountain road and back! They were depending upon me to get them safely there and back, and I could scarcely reach the gas pedal and brakes! I have always been short, and I only weighed 120 pounds. The road seemed one continuous route of sharp, unending curves for MANY miles as we wound our way to the top of that mountain. Going up was hard. Coming down was even harder! I had to literally stand my 120 pounds on the brakes to keep it from careening down the mountain and over a deadly precipice. No power brakes on that bus. A miracle trip indeed!

Being a devout Christian and wanting no hint of impropriety with members of the opposite sex, under the threat of physical harm, I conscripted the only young man on campus who was smaller than me to accompany us. I did not wish to be the only male on that bus! And, to further avoid any hint of impropriety, I

The Depression Pilgrim's Journey
The Man Who Walked through Time

had the host college coordinator provide me with a blanket and pillows, and I slept in the school bus!! This is an account of something that you only wish to do once in a lifetime! Like the Presbyterian who fell down stairs, got up, brushed himself off, and said, "If it was predestined to happen, I'm glad that's over!"

The Depression Pilgrim's Journey
The Man Who Walked through Time

The Rock Altar - 1953

Deep within most of us is a treasured memory, a loved one, a vivid experience, a success story, a special moment, a time of triumph, a special friend, a "first remembered experience", etc. For me, it is a throwback to a simpler time when there was less turmoil, less anger, less uncertainty, more trust, and more faith in God and our fellow man.

It began for me as an early Christian with little guidance except what I found in faithful reading of the Holy Scriptures. I began sharing my faith. I began witnessing in the classroom, on the streets, in jails, in cottage prayer services, and in local churches at their request. I was a teenage speaker on a local radio station (WGAA-1340) and a local television station, WROM-TV (now WTVC9 in Chattanooga), sponsored by others, and soon became a regular evangelistic speaker across the southeastern region. I needed all the help I could muster up. To me, prayer was the key to all the challenges I faced, so I not only spent time in prayer at home, but I also sought privacy and solitude in another isolated location.

In rural Polk County, Georgia, on the Lake Creek Road toward the U.S Highway 27 South, past the railroad tracks on the right, up a winding footpath and gentle slope to an opening in the wooded hillside was an ideal place of privacy and solitude. This isolated

The Depression Pilgrim's Journey
The Man Who Walked through Time

location was just the place to commune with God. As I regularly walked up this pathway, I would reach down and pick up a small stone from among the many rocks along the winding path, and upon reaching the top, I would lay it there in a neat pile as a reminder of my visit. After a while, I invited acquaintances to join me in a season of prayer who would also pick up a stone and do likewise as they joined me in prayer. In the years that followed, that pile of stones grew into a very large area of many feet in diameter and several feet tall! I called it "The Rock Altar".

The night I graduated High School, it was a new beginning. There is a reason it is called "Commencement". Although I was valedictorian of my graduating class, I still felt the need for knowledge I did not yet have. I needed wisdom that only comes from God, and with time, the application of that knowledge. Rather than join my classmates in a time of celebration, I slipped out quietly and spent the entire night at the rock altar seeking guidance for the journey ahead. I needed that assurance. For me, it has been an anchor through uncharted and troubled waters.

To this day, that "Rock Altar" remains one of my most treasured memories.

The Depression Pilgrim's Journey
The Man Who Walked through Time

End of Chapter

Chapter 3
The Later Years
No Regrets

It's human nature to seek the easy way.

My impoverished, destitute, and hopeless plight would easily have provided cover for the "victim mentality".

It would have been so easy to blame the situation on "circumstances" and give up.

But I chose to use the situation blockades as "Stepping stones" and to "lift myself up" above the circumstances!

I chose to think of not what I was missing… but what I was escaping!

I will address later how I qualified to become a psychologist in 1963, tested over 20,000 and counseled thousands as a Pastor and counselor.

My experience as a counselor for many decades is that: the thing that torments people most is the baggage of "regrets," and the hardest thing is to forgive oneself.

There is no such thing as a neutral influence!

The Depression Pilgrim's Journey
The Man Who Walked through Time

The Depression Pilgrim's Journey
The Man Who Walked through Time

FT. MCCLELLAN 1955

PAUL & LARRY

Paul & Brother, Larry
Prior to expected deployment

The Depression Pilgrim's Journey
The Man Who Walked through Time

Pastor, Evangelist, Educator, Counselor, and Computer Pioneer:

How did I come to have a multiple-track career as a teacher, Pastor, evangelist, counselor, consultant, and computer pioneer? This will explain how that originated.

When I graduated from high school, I was drafted into class 1A, and no one would hire me. Everywhere I applied, they would all say, "We would love to have you, but we are at war, and they are going to draft you and turn you into a target. You are going to die on some foreign battlefield. But, if you survive the war, come back, and we will immediately have a place for you." That led nowhere.

In desperation, I filled out an application with the Georgia State Employment Office. I received a card in the mail to come for an interview. I went as directed and was greeted by three well-dressed men who identified themselves as IBM executives from the White Plains and Poughkeepsie, NY offices, looking for a male in the South willing to work for a female.

In those days, only females worked in automatic data processing in industry, which consisted of punched-card processing equipment. Females generally have a greater sustained attention span than most males. After normal pleasantries, one of the executives said to me, "Are you willing to work for a female?"

The Depression Pilgrim's Journey
The Man Who Walked through Time

I thought that rather odd, and I replied, "I would have no problem with that. My mother is a female. My sister is a female. I have a girlfriend who is a female. I like girls!"

He said, "You're hired!"

They arranged for me to go to their several educational centers to learn how to wire control boards for their punched-card tabulating, collating, and calculating machines. I also spent some time keyboarding information into 80-column punched cards on a Key Punch machine. The first business computer was installed in the U.S. Census Bureau. It was not an IBM. The second one I was told was an IBM. I then got into the fray of computing machines in industry, not only as a computer pioneer, but I was also told that I was the first male to work in industry in automatic data processing.

I am also a published Poet and Author. Included in a number of professional books of Poetry, including: International Library of Poetry (1999) and Famous Poets of the Heartland (2010). My 1st book (1970-1973) was a scientific treatise using inferential statistics to prove my thesis. My 2nd book (2021-2022) was at the urging of my deceased spouse and soul mate. It is a selection of Gospel Message outlines developed by me over several decades in the ministry across the Southeast (MS, AL, GA, FL, VA, WV, SC, NC,

The Depression Pilgrim's Journey
The Man Who Walked through Time

KY, OH) on live radio and TV, and provided DVDs. The 2nd book is in the public domain since 2022 as "Re-Joyce" in her honor.

This gives a thumbnail sketch of how that unlikely combination came about. It led to a storied journey in an otherwise bleak future for a "southern plowboy" born into abject poverty.

The greatest joy and reward in my life is as a witness for the Lord Jesus: on the streets, in the jails, in the military, in the marketplace, in the workplace, in the corporate boardroom, in the pulpit and in the college classrooms as a self-supporting missionary where I molded and shaped "living messages" which I sent to the future! It served as a Church without walls and without role-expectations, where I won students to the Lord Jesus; performed their weddings and renewal of vows; and, when deceased, conducted their funerals. It's been a blessed pilgrimage, and I have enjoyed the journey!

But, I long to return to that simpler time; to breathe the clean country air; to inebriate on the aroma of new-mown hay; to count the stars at dusk; to slumber to the bird's lullaby; to awaken to the eagle's call; and to commune with God away from the crime and stench of the city.

But, alas, I'll have to await the New Jerusalem!

The Depression Pilgrim's Journey
The Man Who Walked through Time

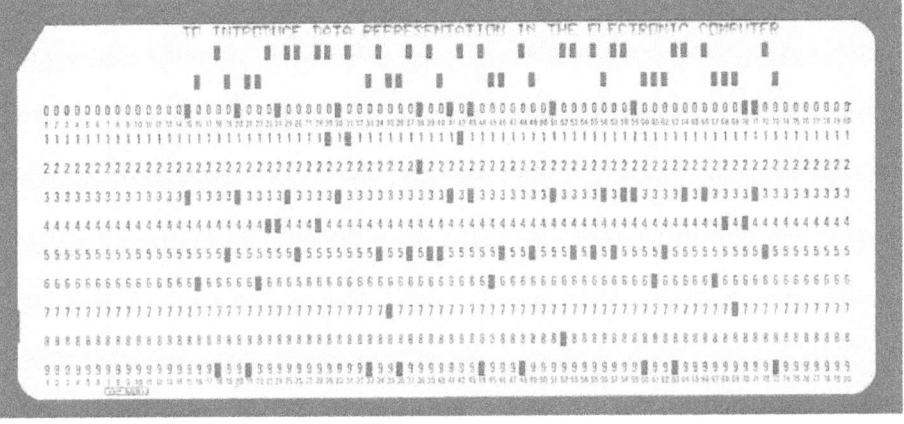

The Depression Pilgrim's Journey
The Man Who Walked through Time

This is to Certify

that _Paul Alton Kitch_

who has given evidence that he possesses gifts for the work of

The Gospel Ministry

was _Licensed_ to preach the Gospel as he may have opportunity, and to exercise his gifts in the work of the Ministry

by _Lake Creek Baptist_ Church

at _Cedartown, Ga RFD 2_

on the _24_ day of _June_, 19_51_

Harvey C Brown
Pastor

Lewis Drummond
Clerk

The Depression Pilgrim's Journey
The Man Who Walked through Time

Certificate of Ordination

We, the undersigned, hereby certify that upon the recommendation and request of the Salem Baptist Church at Bluffton, Alabama, which had full and sufficient opportunity for judging of his gifts, and after satisfactory examination by us in regard to his Christian experience, call to the ministry, and views of Bible Doctrine,

Paul Fitch

was solemnly and publicly set apart and ordained to the work of The Gospel Ministry by authority and order of the Lake Creek Baptist Church at Route 2, Johnstown, on the 24 day of Oct., 1954.

Ordaining Council — Harry C. Brown, Moderator

[signatures of ordaining council members and roles]

The Depression Pilgrim's Journey
The Man Who Walked through Time

The Depression Pilgrim's Journey
The Man Who Walked through Time

ARMY EXTENSION COURSES

Certificate of Completion of Course Series

This is to certify, That CORPORAL PAUL A. RITCH, 24 774 669, INF-NG
COMPANY "B", 163RD TANK BATTALION, GEORGIA NATIONAL GUARD has successfully
completed the TEN series,
Extension Courses, of the INFANTRY SCHOOL
(19 55-19 56 Announcement) with a rating of EXCELLENT credit 244

Date 14 FEBRUARY, 19 56

RUSSELL S. PRICE
Lt Col, Infantry
Deputy Director for AEC

[SEAL]   APPROVED:

FOR THE COMMANDANT:

LEO D. WELTSCH
Captain, Infantry
Actg Asst Adj Gen

WD AGO FORM 152   PREVIOUS EDITIONS OF THIS FORM ARE OBSOLETE

The Depression Pilgrim's Journey
The Man Who Walked through Time

An Exit Ramp to a Roadside Revival

The year was 1956. The place was somewhere south of Atlanta, Georgia. The occasion was my returning to Ft Benning, Georgia.

Returning to duty at Ft Benning, GA, on a July Sunday morning in 1956, I kept looking for an exit sign pointing to a Church where I could stop and worship. I was in full military dress uniform since I had to report back by 4:00 p.m.

At length, somewhere south of Atlanta, GA, I spotted a sign of a Baptist Church. Since I had been Pastor of an independent Baptist Church, I exited the highway, found the Church, parked, and went in. The ushers saw my name tag, we exchanged greetings, and I chose a seat in the very back of the Church in order not to be conspicuous.

After the Worship Leader had finished and turned the service over to the Pastor, the Pastor greeted everyone and ceremoniously announced that there was a special guest in the back of the building, and he felt led of the Lord that "Serviceman Ritch" should give the morning message!

Honored, I arose, went forward, took my Bible out of my uniform, read a passage, and began the message. It was from John 3:16. I gave my personal testimony on how the matchless Grace of a loving Creator had given me pardon, peace, provisions, preservation, protections, patience, power, and the promise of a perfect paradise-home. I gave an invitation and over a dozen people came forward, accepted the Lord, and gave their testimonies!

It gave credence to the Scriptural command to: "sanctify the Lord God in your hearts: and be ready always to give an answer to every man that asks you a reason of the hope that is in you with meekness and fear: (1st Peter 3:15) KJV.

God is good!

Amen! And hallelujah

Paul A. Ritch

The Depression Pilgrim's Journey
The Man Who Walked through Time

Paul Army NG Discharge 1956

Honorable Discharge

from the Armed Forces of the United States of America

This is to certify that

Sgt E-5 Paul Allen Ritch, 24 774 069

was Honorably Discharged from the NATIONAL GUARD OF GEORGIA AND AS A RESERVE OF THE ARMY OF THE UNITED STATES on the 18th day of October 1956

This certificate is awarded as a testimonial of Honest and Faithful Service

JAMES J. CARTER
Capt. Armor, GaNG
Commanding

NGB FORM 55
1 JAN 53

The Depression Pilgrim's Journey
The Man Who Walked through Time

NATIONAL GUARD BUREAU
REPORT OF SEPARATION AND RECORD OF SERVICE IN THE ARMY NATIONAL GUARD OF THE UNITED STATES AND THE ARMY NATIONAL GUARD OF GEORGIA
TYPE OF DISCHARGE: HONORABLE
(No erasures or alterations in this entry valid)

1	NAME (Last, first, middle initial)	Ritch, Paul A.
2	SERVICE NO.	24 774 669
3	GRADE	Sgt E5
4	ARM OR SERVICE	Armor
5	TERM OF ENLISTMENT	3 yrs
6	ORGANIZATION	Co. "B" 163rd Tk Bn, GaNG
	HOME STATION	Cedartown, Georgia
7	DATE OF DISCHARGE	18 Oct 56
8	PLACE OF DISCHARGE	Cedartown, Georgia
9	PERMANENT ADDRESS FOR MAILING PURPOSES	104 Dink Ave. Marietta, Georgia
10	DATE OF BIRTH	19 May 35
11	PLACE OF BIRTH	Rome, Georgia
12	CIVILIAN OCCUPATION	Receiving Clerk, Lockheed Aircraft Corp., Marietta, Georgia
13	RACE	White X
14	MARITAL STATUS	Married X
15	U.S. CITIZEN	Yes X
16	COLOR EYES	Blue
17	COLOR HAIR	Blond
18	HEIGHT	5 ft 6 in
19	WEIGHT	132 lbs
20	NO. DEPENDENTS	One (1)

MILITARY HISTORY

21	DATE AND PLACE OF ENLISTMENT	19 Oct 53, Cedartown, Georgia
22	MILITARY OCCUPATIONAL SPECIALTY AND NUMBER	Communications Chief (312.70)
23	MILITARY QUALIFICATION AND DATE	US Rifle M-1 Marksman 2 May 54; Auto-Rifle Cal 30. Expert 27 Aug 55; Pistol Cal. 45 Marksman 3 Jun 56
24	DECORATIONS, CITATIONS, MEDALS, BADGES, COMMENDATIONS, AND CAMPAIGN RIBBONS AWARDED OR AUTHORIZED	None
25	PRIOR SERVICE	None

RETIREMENT CREDITS EARNED (This period of service)

FIRST YEAR			SECOND YEAR			THIRD YEAR			TOTAL POINTS THIS SERVICE
FROM	TO	POINTS	FROM	TO	POINTS	FROM	TO	POINTS	
19 Oct 53	18 Oct 54	75	19 Oct 54	18 Oct 55	74	19 Oct 55	18 Oct 56	75	224

27. LENGTH THIS SERVICE			28. TOTAL SERVICE FOR PAY PURPOSES			29. LATEST IMMUNIZATION DATES				30. HIGHEST GRADE HELD
YEARS	MONTHS	DAYS	YEARS	MONTHS	DAYS	SMALLPOX	TYPHOID	TETANUS	OTHER	
3	0	0	3	0	0	1954	1954	1954	None	Sgt E-5

31. SERVICE SCHOOLS ATTENDED AND DATES: Communications Specialist Crse (312.70) Armored School 20 May 56 to 2 Jun 56 incl.

32. EDUCATION (Years): GRAMMAR 8 | HIGH SCHOOL 4 | COLLEGE None

33. REASON AND AUTHORITY FOR DISCHARGE: Expiration term of service par 6 a, NGR 25-3

34. REMARKS: RECOMMENDED FOR REENLISTMENT

35. SIGNATURE OF PERSON BEING DISCHARGED: Paul A. Ritch

36. SIGNATURE OF OFFICER AUTHORIZED TO SIGN: JAMES J. CARTER, Capt. Armor, Comnd'g

The Depression Pilgrim's Journey
The Man Who Walked through Time

Paul Army NG 2nd LT Clearance 1957

HEADQUARTERS, THIRD UNITED STATES ARMY
Office of the Assistant Chief of Staff, G2
Fort McPherson, Georgia

AJSEC-6.2-G3008074 (G2) Date: 1 August 1957

SUBJECT: Results of Investigation

TO: The Adjutant General
State of Georgia
P. O. Box 4839
Atlanta, Georgia

    1. Reference ltr., your office, File: 201-Ritch, Paul Allen (Enl), Subj: "Request for Investigation of National Guard Personnel", dtd 18 Jun 57.

    2. The indicated type of investigation, which meets the scope outlined in AR 604-5, was completed this date by Headquarters, Third United States Army concerning:

Name: RITCH, Paul Allen   Rank or Grade: 2d Lt
SN or SSN: 24774669 (NG)   DOB: 19 May 35   POB: Silver Creek, Ga.

    a. ( )BACKGROUND INVESTIGATION, (XX)NATIONAL AGENCY CHECK, ( )NATIONAL AGENCY CHECK with written inquiries to determine individual's suitability for access to ( )CONFIDENTIAL, (XX)SECRET, ( )TOP SECRET, ( )CRYPTOLOGIC material.

    b. National Agency Check to determine individual's suitability as an applicant for appointment for ( )SPECIAL REGISTRANT, ( )ROTC, ( )RA, ( )USAR, ( )AUS, ( )OCS, (XX)NG.

    3. No information reflecting adversely upon the loyalty, integrity, trustworthiness, character or discretion of the individual was revealed in the course of this investigation.

    4. Request appropriate entries be made in the personnel records of the individual, as prescribed in paragraph 18, AR 604-5 and change 1, thereto, if applicable.

    5. In the event there has been a change in the status of the individual, request compliance with paragraph 16e, AR 604-5.

FOR THE ASSISTANT CHIEF OF STAFF, G2:

(XX) Incl
DD Form 398 (dupe)

DONALD H. EGAN
Major, MI(Inf)
Control Officer

Copies furnished: PO Box 1736, 699 Ponce de Leon Ave, NE, Atlanta, Ga.

L 470, 27 May 57

The Depression Pilgrim's Journey
The Man Who Walked through Time

Paul Commission Application

SPECIAL REPORT

Section I – Personal Data of Officer Being Rated

Ritch, Paul A. — 84 774 069 — 1 May 56 — Sgt E-5 — Armor

Co B, 163rd Tk Bn, (90MM Gun) GaNG
Cedartown, Georgia

312.70 — Sgt E-5

Communications Chief

Section II – Reason Report Being Rendered

X Applying for Commission

Section III – Description of Rated Officer and Comments

This enlisted man is devoted to the service. He is intelligent and resourceful, and has the mental and physical qualifications necessary to make an excellent officer. He has demonstrated these qualities on a number of occasions. This enlisted man is one of the best instructors that I have ever witnessed.

This enlisted man is physically qualified to perform any duty required by his grade or branch in time of war.

An alert, earnest enlisted man who is most devoted to the service. He is dependable and needs only a minimum of supervision. He will definitely be an asset to this command in his new grade.

13 Nov 57 — JOHN M. GRUBBS, JR. Capt, 0296941, Armor
Co B, 163rd Tk Bn, (90MM Gun) GaNG
Company Commander

10 Dec 57 — HORACE T. CLARY, Lt Col, 0362014, Armor
Hq 163rd Tk Bn, GaNG
Commanding

OFFICER EFFICIENCY REPORT
DA Form 67-4

The Depression Pilgrim's Journey
The Man Who Walked through Time

DATES FROM	TO	STATE OR FEDERAL	STATION	GRADE	ORGANIZATION	DUTY	FULL NAME AND GRADE OF IMMEDIATE COMMANDING OFFICER
19 Oct 53	18 Oct 56	State	Cedartown Georgia	Sgt	Co F, 122d Inf, GaNG	Comm Chief	James J. Carter Captain
19 Oct 56	Present	State	Cedartown Georgia	Sgt	Co B, 163rd Tk Bn, GaNG	Comm Chief	John M. Grubbs, Jr Captain

u. Remarks.-- Any other information you may desire to submit None

v. "I certify that I have read paragraph 2, NGB Circular 28, 22 December 1948, and (have) (have never) engaged in disloyal or subversive activities as defined therein." (Delete and initial word(s) not applicable).

PAUL ALLEN RITCH
(Signature—Give all names in full)
(Sign all copies)

1st INDORSEMENT (Prepared by organization commander)

Commanding Officer, Co B, 163rd Tk Bn, (90MM Gun) GaNG, Cedartown, Ga, 18 Nov 57

Commanding Officer, 163rd Tk Bn, (90MM Gun) GaNG, Calhoun, Georgia.

X Approval recommended. The statements of the applicant have been verified as far as practicable and are considered to be correct.

His appointment is desired to fill the position of 2nd Lt, Cml Platoon Leader (1203) vice Original Vacancy

(Sign all copies) JOHN M. GRUBBS, Jr, Capt, Armor, GaNG, Commanding

2d Ind INDORSEMENT (Prepared by regimental or corresponding commander)

Headquarters 163rd Tank Bn, 90MM, GaNG, Calhoun, Georgia, 10 Dec 57

TO: The Adjutant General, State of Georgia, Atlanta, Ga.

True Approval recommended.

(Sign all copies) HORACE T. CLARY, Lt Col Commanding Armor, GaNG

The Depression Pilgrim's Journey
The Man Who Walked through Time

Paul Mt Oliver, Pastor 1963

Paul Mt Oliver, Pastor 1964

The Depression Pilgrim's Journey
The Man Who Walked through Time

A Working Evangelist

In those earlier days, I was speaking on local live radio WGAA-1340 in Cedartown, Georgia, and live TV on WROM-TV in Rome, Georgia (now WTVC-9 in Chattanooga, Tennessee). Times were hard, and evangelizing was done basically at one's own expense. So, I was a working evangelist. I had been recruited by IBM as a male and trained to work in a female-dominated profession, and I was gainfully employed as a computer professional at a carpet mill in Dalton, Georgia, to create the first custom-designed computer system for the carpet industry. Things were going great, and IBM brought curious businessmen from Europe to see it! That was in 1965.

Tennessee was planning the first post-high-school, two-year degree-granting institution as Chattanooga State Technical Institute (CSTI). One of the Steering Committee Members was a friend named Earl Geer. He recommended me to the founding Director, and I was recruited to teach Computer Science at CSTI. With recruited faculty, I developed the world's first academic program in Computer Science. I was able to get the prestigious accreditation by the Engineers Council for Professional Development (ECPD). With the help of a government grant in 1969, I secured an IBM 360 computer system and was the founding Director of the Computer Center. While also teaching Computer

The Depression Pilgrim's Journey
The Man Who Walked through Time

Science, I custom-programmed the system to take care of student registration, grade reporting, payroll, cost accounting, inventory, and other miscellaneous needs of the Institute. Later, the Institute was converted to Chattanooga State Technical Community College (CSTCC). Current CSTCC President Dr. Rebecca Ashford named the Data Center in my honor.

I got the Institute approved as a testing site for various professions, including accountants, engineers, and others. And, I worked with the Educational Testing Service on the College Level Examination Program (CLEP) standardized tests.

I was appointed to be the Articulating Representative to the following Tennessee educational governing bodies:

1. The State University and Community College System of Tennessee (SUCCST).

2. The Tennessee Land Grant University main campus at Knoxville.

3. The Tennessee Higher Education Commission of Tennessee (THEC).

These busy years also led to pursuing a number of advanced degrees while also conducting protracted evangelical services across the southeast, including MS, AL, GA, FL, TN, VA, WV, SC,

The Depression Pilgrim's Journey
The Man Who Walked through Time

NC, KY, and OH on live radio and live TV, and at times provided DVDs.

And now, with a terminal degree in Management, I have developed Management Programs for governments, industries, and educational institutions.

The Depression Pilgrim's Journey
The Man Who Walked through Time

Car in my reserved parking space

The year was 1965. The place was Dalton (Whitfield County), Georgia.

The issue was a violation of reserved parking.

As I returned from lunch one day in 1965, a General Motors car was parked in my reserved parking space at the main entrance to the offices of Modern Carpet Industries in Dalton, Georgia. I parked, went inside, and inquired if anyone knew who it might be, and no one seemed to know. I reflected upon the situation and thought of a plan.

I had kept a spare key of every car I had ever owned. I had them in the trunk of my car. I had been advised by a friend who had been VP of a Motor Company that the limited space on a key made it very likely that, on average, a key from the same manufacturer would likely open the door to many cars from that same manufacturer, EXCEPT the same color as your car.

I went to my car, retrieved the spare keys, isolated the General Motors car keys, and the third key opened the offending car! I got out my handkerchief to grip the steering wheel; cranked the car and drove it several blocks away; parked and locked it; wiped away all prints; and walked back to my office.

The Depression Pilgrim's Journey
The Man Who Walked through Time

The local Sheriff was a good friend of mine. I called him and told him what I had done so that when he got the report of a stolen car, he would know how to deal with it. He thought it was hilarious! I asked him to never tell the owner how his car got relocated. He promised.

I suspect the owner died wondering how his car got relocated, locked, and nothing missing!

The Depression Pilgrim's Journey
The Man Who Walked through Time

Paul and CSTI IBM 1620 1967

The Depression Pilgrim's Journey
The Man Who Walked through Time

Additional Memory Salesman 1969

IBM

International Business Machines Corporation

801 McCallie Avenue
Chattanooga, Tennessee 37403
615/267-9571

January 30, 1969

Mr. Paul A. Ritch
Chattanooga State Technical Institute
4501 Amnicola Highway
Chattanooga, Tennessee

Dear Paul

Thank you for your letter of January 20. The equipment specified in your letter will have a purchase price as follows:

    Add'l 32K Core $54,420.00
    Field Installation
        Charge   255.00

These prices are subject to applicable educational allowances. As we discussed, there is a question as to whether the FIC is subject to EA. As soon as I have a clarification I will let you know.

As you instructed, we have requested installation the first week in August.

                Sincerely,

                Jack

                Jack D. Brock, Jr.
                Marketing Representative

JDB:Jr./bh

The Depression Pilgrim's Journey
The Man Who Walked through Time
Additional Memory Manager 1969

International Business Machines Corporation

801 McCallie Avenue
Chattanooga, Tennessee 37403
615/267-9611

February 19, 1969

Mr. Paul Ritch
Chattanooga State Technical Institute
Post Office Box 670
Chattanooga, Tennessee 37401

Dear Paul:

Thank you for your letter ordering a model change from Mod. E to Mod F for your 2030-17988.

The purchase price for this feature is $54,420.00, plus installation charges, and consists in part of used components which are warranted equivalent to new in performance when properly installed in an IBM machine.

Thank you again for placing this order with our company.

Yours very truly,

C. V. Bryant
Branch Manager

CVB:sb

The Depression Pilgrim's Journey
The Man Who Walked through Time

Paul CSTI Office 1970

The Depression Pilgrim's Journey
The Man Who Walked through Time
Paul Content Winner Seymour Freely 1970

EDITORS' FOOTNOTES

The Name Game: Meet Seymour Freely, Our Dusty Chancellor

Last June in this column we requested that administrators "put aside your problems for a minute, think up some brilliant suggestions . . ." for naming our new cartoon character (see p. 21). Eighty-four administrators did and the result was 183 separate names.

C&UB editors, in a round of judging, finally decided that the name "Seymour Freely," submitted by Paul A. Ritch, head of computer science and management information technology at Chattanooga State Technological Institute, most aptly described the nuances of his character which the editors wanted. The contest was also opened to McGraw-Hill employes, and Charles A. Goehring in Novato, Calif., came up with the name "The Dusty Chancellor," which the editors thought appropriate for the cartoon strip's permanent title. Original color cartoons by Jay Lynch have been sent to both Mr. Ritch and Mr. Goehring.

Almost a dozen people wanted to name him "Cub" or Cubby," after the magazine and/or the place where he stores things ("cubby-hole, get it?" said one). Others saw only Seymour's occupation and failed to look into his full character: "Willy Sudzemstuff," wrote one; "Old Slosher," "Captain Clean," "Germ Jockey," suggested others.

Some readers perceived Seymour as having greater dimensions, however, suggesting "Phil Ossufur," "Noah Lott," "Gene Yuss," "P. H. Dee" and "Cub Laudey." In fact, one contributor thought a new discipline could be created for him so he could be a "Doctor of Broomology."

One contributor, who perhaps had an Earth Day meeting on his campus, thought our special janitor should be named "Pfc. E. Cology." And another with contemporary insight recommended "Sy Lentmajorski."

You can't go far in American humor without some mention of ethnic considerations, so . . . "Ollie the Yanitor," "Svenson the Svepper," "Janitwart," and "Scrub D'Flores"??

A "name which would be an acrostic is MECO, indicating Maintenance Engineer's Campus Observation," wrote one reader. Another suggested "Concierge" from the Latin meaning "fellow slave," adding, "Aren't we all?"

Another contributor drew an analogy to the movie "Charly," suggesting the name "Algernon, after the uniquely named little creature (a mouse) who did not achieve very much notoriety for his instinctive efforts." Even a bit of sentimentality crept into the name game: "I offer the name Jerry in honor of our janitor in high school, class of 1931," wrote one reader (Jerry wrote in her yearbook, "When you're married and washing dishes, think of Jerry and his good wishes").

It was all a lot of fun, but we're not likely to suggest again soon that our readers "put aside your problems for a minute, think up some brilliant suggestions . . ."

The Depression Pilgrim's Journey
The Man Who Walked through Time

Paul Seymour Freely Winner 1970

COLLEGE & UNIVERSITY BUSINESS · 1050 Merchandise Mart · Chicago, Illinois 60654 · (312) 467-6700

August 17, 1970

Mr. Paul A. Ritch
1634 Mary DuPre Drive
Chattanooga, Tenn. 37421

Dear Mr. Ritch:

We have just completed the "What's-His-Name?" contest for the new cartoon strip we will inaugurate in the September issue of College & University Business. It is my pleasure to inform you, on behalf of the C&UB staff, that your entry "Seymore Freely" was selected as our character's new name (although we changed it slightly to Seymour Freely).

A large, original color drawing of Seymour has been mailed to you under separate cover. I am certain you will find it attractively framed and executed.

Thanks for giving Seymour his name and for participating in C&UB. Incidentally, we are titling the strip "The Dusty Chancellor."

Sincerely,

Dennis W. Binning
Editor-In-Chief

DWB/mr

The Depression Pilgrim's Journey
The Man Who Walked through Time
Paul National Contest Winner Seymour Freely 1970

The Depression Pilgrim's Journey
The Man Who Walked through Time

Paul Presenting CSTI Graduate Degrees

The Depression Pilgrim's Journey
The Man Who Walked through Time

Trena First Enrollee CSTI Secretarial Science

With State Board approval for the Secretarial Science Program, funds for equipment and faculty, I bought equipment, hired faculty, and WAITED several months to offer the program until Trena graduated High School and could be the 1st student!

The Depression Pilgrim's Journey
The Man Who Walked through Time

Paul Articulating Rep to SUCCST 1975

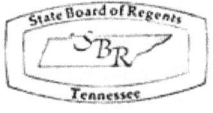

**The State University
and Community College System of Tennessee**
1 Park Plaza • Nashville, Tennessee 37203

January 24, 1975

Dr. Paul A. Ritch
Chattanooga State Technical Community College
4501 Amnicola Highway
Chattanooga, Tennessee 37406

Dear Dr. Ritch:

As you know, you have been designated by the president of your institution to serve as a member of the <u>Ad Hoc</u> Articulation Committee of the SUCCST. The purpose of this committee initially will be as follows:

1. To begin looking at some of the problems of articulation in the System.

2. To share ideas as to how solutions of the problems may be reached.

3. To develop a general agreement of articulation.

4. To develop a system of communication and a working relationship between institutions of the System for resolving difference of interpretation which directly effect students as groups and as individuals.

The efforts of this committee will compliment and supplement the work already done by other system-wide committees on articulation. However, during the early stages the committee will focus on the institutions of our system.

Our offices will be setting a time and date of the first committee meeting within the next two weeks at which time members of the committee will be notified. Please feel free to call or write should you have any questions on this matter.

Sincerely yours,

C. C. Humphreys
Chancellor

The Depression Pilgrim's Journey
The Man Who Walked through Time

PAR with the co-developer of the world's 1st computer

Some years ago I had the honor of spending the day with the co-developer of the world's first computer (the ENIAC I), and the Director of the USAF Institute of Technology. We three, identified below, were the featured speakers at the International Association of Accountants' annual meeting. Dr. Eckert to tell the attendees how it was "then"; I to tell them how it was "now"1 and, Dr. Demidovich to tell them that we may sleep securely at night, knowing how the USAF and NORAD use computers buried deep in the Colorado Mountains to scan, log, and intervemne for the security of the USA.

We were on the platform together, heard each other speak, and spent the day together. It was one of the greatest honors ever afforded me.

From left to right in the photo below:

• Dr. John Demidovich, Director of the USAF Institute of Technology.

• Dr. J. Presper Eckert, co-developer of the world's first computer, the ENIAC I (Electrical Numerical Integrator and Calculator).

Dr. John Presper Eckert and Dr. John W. Mauchly built the world's first computer at the University of Pennsylvania in the mid-nineteen forties.

The Depression Pilgrim's Journey
The Man Who Walked through Time

• Dr. Paul A. Ritch, representing Computer Technologies for Tennessee. The 1st computer for non-military use was in the U.S. Census Bureau (1951); the 2nd in the GE Appliance Park (KY) in the early fifties. The 3rd and succeeding ones came after I enter the field.

Paul A. Ritch

Paul with Dr. Prespert Exckert

The Depression Pilgrim's Journey
The Man Who Walked through Time
Paul Certified Manager 1980

Institute of Certified Professional Managers

Dear Dr. Roth,

Congratulations! You have passed all three parts of the examination and are now a Certified Manager. Your name will be submitted to the Board of Regents for formal approval at their June meeting. Sometime thereafter, you will receive your certificate, along with a "Code of Ethics" and a formal letter of congratulations from the Executive Director of the Institute. Until that time, please consider this as official notification of your outstanding achievement. Once again, congratulations.

Cordially,

Nancy E. Fox

Nancy E. Fox
Administrative Assistant

The Depression Pilgrim's Journey
The Man Who Walked through Time

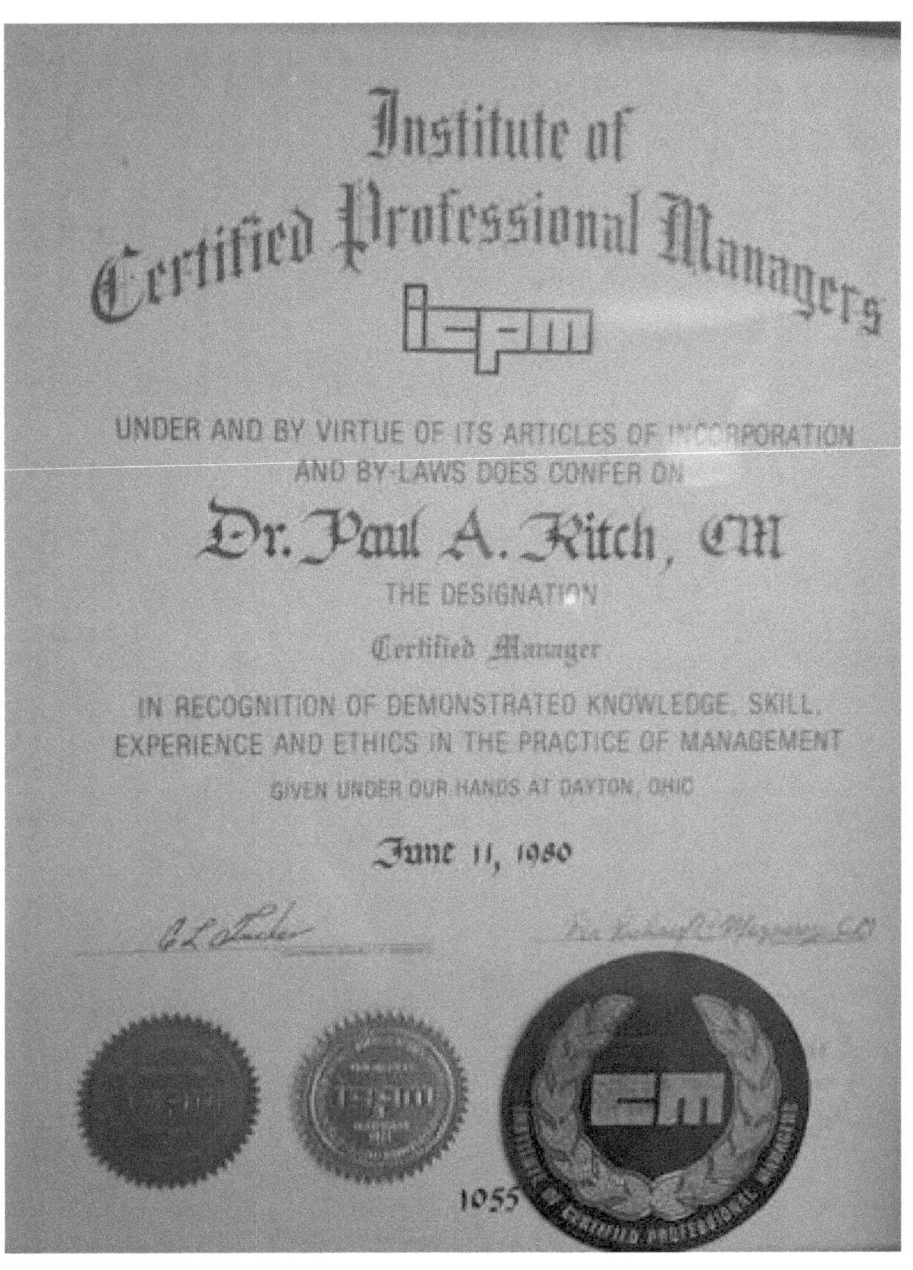

The Depression Pilgrim's Journey
The Man Who Walked through Time

Joyce's Surprise 60th Birthday Party 09/21/1991

Attendees

Family

Joyce & Paul

The Depression Pilgrim's Journey
The Man Who Walked through Time

Paul and Joyce Plains, GA 1998

President Jimmy Carter & Rosalynn Carter
Joyce Ann Ritch & Paul A. Ritch
Maranatha Baptist Church; Plains, GA
Sunday 05/31/98

The Depression Pilgrim's Journey
The Man Who Walked through Time

Paul A. Ritch 2006

The Depression Pilgrim's Journey
The Man Who Walked through Time

Paul A. Ritch 2010

The Depression Pilgrim's Journey
The Man Who Walked through Time

CSTCC Data Center Dedication (1) 2018

You're Invited!

Please join Dr. Rebecca Ashford,
President of Chattanooga State Community College,
on Saturday, September 8, 2018 from 2-4 p.m.
for a reception and special dedication of the
Dr. Paul A. Ritch Data Center

Dr. Ritch is a founding faculty member of the college who
established the data center.

Please **RSVP** by September 5th.

The Depression Pilgrim's Journey
The Man Who Walked through Time

CSTCC Data Center Dedication (2) 2018

Dr. Paul A. Ritch Data Center

Dedicated on: September 8, 2018

The Depression Pilgrim's Journey
The Man Who Walked through Time

CSTCC Students at Dedication

Paul CSTCC Dedication

CSTCC Data Center Dedication Plaque

The Depression Pilgrim's Journey
The Man Who Walked through Time

Paul Honor CSTCC 2018

Dr. Paul A. Ritch honored by Tennessee College he helped establish

Dr. Paul A. Ritch, native of Polk County, Georgia and graduate & valedictorian of the Cedartown High Class of 1953, for more than sixty-five years has been a computer pioneer, pastor (12 years), evangelist (53 years), educator, counselor, psychologist, and keynote speaker for a number of national conventions, one as co-keynote speaker with the computer pioneer Dr. J. Presper Eckert who built the world's first programmable computer called the ENIAC. More recently, he has been simulcasting Gospel messages ("Re-Joyce") on Sinclair Broadcast Group's 44 regional TV stations in honor of Jesus and his beloved deceased spouse, Joyce Ann Price Ritch. Born into poverty, he applied himself, worked hard, studied long and lifted himself out of the impoverished conditions into which he was born. He was recruited into industrial data processing before the computer got into it, sent to the numerous IBM Educational Centers in major U. S. cities to prepare him for the computer seen coming on the industrial horizon. The first computer for general use was installed in the U. S. Census Bureau. Industrial use would soon follow. Dr. Ritch was recently honored by the Tennessee College he helped establish.

Equipped with the previously noted unique exposure and training, he developed the world's first computerized system for the carpet industry in Dalton, Georgia which was visited by representatives from abroad; and, was then recruited to help pioneer technical education in Tennessee and to help establish the "first post-high-school, two-year, degree-granting-institution in Tennessee" (the Chattanooga State Technical Institute, now Chattanooga State Community College). In that capacity, in addition to teaching computer science, he was tapped to establish the first Computer Center. He designed the unique space and environmental requirements for the then leading-edge, state-of-the-art, massive million-dollar IBM-360 computing system and programmed it for use in training computer programmers as well as institutional administrative needs. With faculty, he helped achieve regional accreditation by the Southern Association of Colleges and Schools (SACS), and then with faculty developed the world's first academic program in Computer Science which received prestigious national accreditation by the Engineers Council for Professional Development (ECPD). In a "church without walls", he viewed the students as "living messages" which he was sending to the future. He taught them; he counseled them. When they married, he married them, later renewing vows; and, when they died, he buried them. He impacted them in positive ways (there is no such thing as a "neutral influence"). In alumni reunions, he learned his report card as a professor came in . . . and he passed!

As an adjunct professor, he also taught computer science for the University of Tennessee at Chattanooga and the flagship University of Tennessee in Knoxville. For two years in a row he was International Data Processing Management Association's (DPMA) USA Region-7 (AL, FL, GA, SC, TN) "Computer Sciences Man-of-the-Year". And, he was the College Articulating Rep to the State University & Community College System of TN, the UT System, and the Tennessee Higher Education Council (THEC).

Now, with leading-edge systems for a 150 acre campus and more than 12,000 students, at a special reception and dedication, on September 8, 2018, the College President, Dr. Rebecca Ashford, dedicated the complex as the Chattanooga State "Dr. Paul A. Ritch Data Center".

Autumn 2018: Paul A. Ritch, BA(x3), BB, ThG, MDiv (equiv), MEd, PhD(x2), CDP, CDE, CCP, CM, LPI

The Depression Pilgrim's Journey
The Man Who Walked through Time

Joyce's Mausoleum

Dr WH King, Trena, Tim, Paul

The Depression Pilgrim's Journey
The Man Who Walked through Time

Paul DD214 Destroyed in Fire 2022

NATIONAL PERSONNEL RECORDS CENTER

NATIONAL ARCHIVES

September 14, 2022

PAUL RITCH
1634 MARY DUPRE DR
CHATTANOOGA, TN 37421

RE: Veteran's Name: RITCH, Paul A
        SSN/SN: ******076
        Request Number: 2-23749192845

Dear Recipient:

Thank you for contacting the National Personnel Records Center. The record needed to answer your inquiry is not in our files. If the record were here on July 12, 1973, it would have been in the area that suffered the most damage in the fire on that date and may have been destroyed. The fire destroyed the major portion of records of Army military personnel for the period 1912 through 1959, and records of Air Force personnel with surnames Hubbard through Z for the period 1947 through 1963. Fortunately, there are alternate records sources that often contain information which can be used to reconstruct service record data lost in the fire; however, complete records cannot be reconstructed.

The National Guard record to which you refer is not on file at this Center. National Guard records are normally maintained by the military service or the Adjutant General's Office in the state in which service was performed. Occasionally, portions of these records are transferred to our Center for permanent storage. However, a thorough search of the records finding media at this Center failed to show a record location for the service member. We suggest that you contact the appropriate office listed below for further assistance in locating the desired records.

ARMY NATIONAL GUARD	CONTACT
All	The Adjutant General (of the appropriate state, DC, or Puerto Rico) This website lists Adjutant General contact information: http://www.nationalguard.mil/Resources/StateWebsites.aspx
AIR NATIONAL GUARD	**CONTACT**
National Guard records for service not listed below.	The Adjutant General (of the appropriate state, DC, or Puerto Rico) This website lists Adjutant General contact information: http://www.nationalguard.mil/Resources/StateWebsites.aspx

The Depression Pilgrim's Journey
The Man Who Walked through Time

National Guard members currently on active duty in the Air Force	Air Force Personnel Center HQ AFPC/DPSIRP 550 C Street W JBSA-Randolph AFB, TX 78150-4721
Current National Guard officers not on active duty in the Air Force, or National Guard released from active duty in the Air Force	Air Reserve Personnel Center 18420 E Silver Creek Ave., Bldg 390 MS 68 Buckley AFB, CO 80011

If you have questions or comments regarding this response, you may contact us at 314-801-0800 or by mail at the address shown in the letterhead above. If you contact us, please reference the Request Number listed above. If you are a veteran, or a deceased veteran's next of kin, please consider submitting your future requests online by visiting us at http://vetrecs.archives.gov.

Sincerely,

JOHN WELSH
Expert Archives Technician (AFN-MC2C)

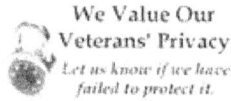
We Value Our Veterans' Privacy
Let us know if we have failed to protect it.

Please complete our on-line survey. We really want to know how we did answering your request. Go to www.archives.gov/veterans/survey and enter your request number 2-23749192845. The survey should only take a few minutes and is used to help improve service to our customers.

The Depression Pilgrim's Journey
The Man Who Walked through Time

End of Chapter

Chapter 4
The Golden Years
The Providential Purpose and Plan in Pain
(Versus, how we deal with it)

I was asked by many to write down how I dealt with the passing of my devoted bride, prayer partner, and best friend of more than half a century. Of the many thousands I have known across the breadth of our journeys, we were more truly "one' than any couple I have ever known. One cannot grasp the magnitude of the pain of that mind-numbing journey without having actually said goodbye to their soul mate. I cared for Joyce Ann 24/7 in the home she made, and I watched her slowly die over a period of four years with nine life-threatening issues, any one of which alone would have taken her home. I then held her Parkinson's trembling hand with one of mine and brushed her lovely hair with the other while she made the transition in the Hospice Crisis Center, and most of me died with her. I felt the life sucked out of me as she breathed her last. I then placed my hand upon her brow, prayed with her, and committed her to the Father's care. Then, with one foot still on this earth and the other trying to follow her, I asked to also be with her and Jesus. For a reason or reasons which I do not fully understand, the Lord chose to leave me here. Perhaps to continue the team ministry she and I had faithfully done for decades, or to share comfort with those who are walking the same journey. In a

The Depression Pilgrim's Journey
The Man Who Walked through Time

life of many decades filled with overwhelming struggles, this has been the most challenging of my human journey.

Pain is prevalent in our human journey. Why then pain? Is there a plan or Providential purpose in our suffering? From the time we are born we all experience pain at some level: a skinned knee as a child, a dissolved friendship, a broken heart as a teenager feeling love for the first time, a failed experience at school or at work, financial reverses, bankruptcy, changes in any form that disturbed our familiar routine or 'security', or the death of a loved one. All of these leave us changed, challenged, and questioning at some point. To understand this perplexing problem, we need to view pain through the lens of eternity rather than this "jar of clay" in which we are imprisoned by time and mortality with a limited vision of the long term. It is hard for us to put our mortal arms around the reality of eternity.

"Death is that beast that has stalked humanity for all time since Adam. "Wherefore, as by one man sin entered into the world, and death by sin; and so death passed upon all men, for that all have sinned" (Rom. 5:12). Death is the predator; you are the prey. It hunts you down. For some, it nibbles away bit by bit. For some, it swallows you up in one bite. For the rest, it stalks us ... relentlessly!

How then do we deal with it and the inevitable?

The Depression Pilgrim's Journey
The Man Who Walked through Time

It has been said that the great historian, Arnold Toynbee, felt that the challenges and the response to those challenges caused civilization to survive and prosper; otherwise, civilization may have died in the Mesopotamian Valley (re: his "challenge/response" theory and his works on the rise and fall of civilizations).

It is my opinion that, if Sherman had not burned Atlanta, it would not have become the metropolitan center of the South. Otherwise, it would have been Chattanooga, which is really the crossroads of the southern United States. Railways, waterways, etc., make Chattanooga the perfect candidate, but it was Atlanta's response to the devastation that stirred it to "rise from the ashes like the phoenix bird" to become the center of the South.

If a woman did not experience the pangs of childbirth, she would not know the joy that follows... "A woman when she is in travail hath sorrow, because her hour is come: but as soon as she is delivered of the child, she remembers no more the anguish, for joy that a man is born into the world" (John 16:21 KJV).

If we had not had the long years of testing, we would not have known the peace that surpasses all understanding that comes with His presence! (Phil. 4:7; Mt. 11:28 "Come unto Me ...").

Diamonds form from temperatures of 2000+ degrees F and pressure of the earth's mantle, some ninety miles below the surface

The Depression Pilgrim's Journey
The Man Who Walked through Time

(rather than from coal, which is rarely below 2 miles deep). And, it is the pressures of life that squeeze out the impurities to make us fit subjects.

We need the clouds and the rains to provide the fruitful yields that sustain life and provide the beautiful flowers that become "candy to the eyes". As a youngster, I was told that if we had only sunshine all the time, then we would have only a desert.

As in all life's challenges, since early adolescence, I have turned to the Holy Scriptures for answers, comfort, and consolation. For instance, I have observed that:

- If Adam had not known the wound in his side, he would not have known the companionship of Eve (Gen.2:21-23).

- If Jacob had not wrestled with the angel until his thigh was out of joint, he may not have had a name change to Israel and with it all the promised blessings given to him (Gen. 32:24-31).

- If Joseph had not been betrayed by his brothers, sold into slavery, and then spent time in a Potipher's dungeon, he would not have been 2nd in command in Egypt (Gen. 37:23-28; 39:20-23; 41:39-41).

- If Moses had not been reared in a Palace and then spent forty years in the desert, he may not have led the Hebrews from bondage (Ex.2:5-10; 3:1-14; 12:31-38).

The Depression Pilgrim's Journey
The Man Who Walked through Time

- If Joshua had voted with the majority of the Canaanite spies, he may not have been the great leader in the conquest of Canaan (Num.14:6-9).

- If Jonah had not spent three days in "Whale University", he would not have known the experience of an entire city of Nineveh turning to the Lord (Jonah 3:1-10).

- If David the shepherd boy had not done battle with Goliath, he may not have gained fame and then ultimately become the king (I Sam.16:1-13; 17:40-51).

- If Daniel had not spent a night in the "Lion's Den Hotel", he likely would not have become Prime Minister of two world empires (Dan.6:16-28).

- If Nehemiah had not been heckled by Sanballat and Tobiah, he might not have prevailed to rebuild the Jerusalem wall (Neh. 4:1-3).

- If Jeremiah had not spent time in a dungeon, he may not have become the great 'weeping prophet' (Jer.38:6).

- If Job had not lost ALL, he would not have known the joy of his latter end, which was better than the beginning (Job 1:13-21; 42:12)

The Depression Pilgrim's Journey
The Man Who Walked through Time

- If John had not been banished to Patmos, he would not have known the joy of the "Revelation of Jesus Christ" (Rev. 1:1), and the vision of the past/present/FUTURE of the Church.

- If Jesus had not known the agony of Gethsemane and the cruel nails of Calvary, He would not have known the triumph of the empty tomb and the "Joy" of the Gentile Church (Hebrews 12:2)

The Depression Pilgrim's Journey
The Man Who Walked through Time

In Loving Memory of Joyce Ann Price Ritch
09/22/1931 – 07/15/2017

½ page in News Free Press Obits in honor of Joyce

Sweetheart, I miss you more than words can express. I have loved you with an unconditional love. I loved you, not only for what you were, but for what I was when I was with you. I loved you because you did more than any creed could ever do to make me better and more than any fate or destiny could ever do to make me happy. You gave me what men long for, seek, die, and never find, and that is total fulfillment! We shared life. We were truly "one". I held your hand while you made the transition, and most of me died with you. And now, without you, what is left of me is a mind-numbing and lonely journey of many challenges. I'm like a half-pair of scissors, and nothing tastes!

Two strokes, Parkinson's, life-threatening COPD and asthma, crippling neuropathy, alternating Hashimoto's and Graves' diseases, Shy-Drager syndrome, vasovagal syncope, gastroparesis, deafness, macular degeneration and fading eyesight, Alzheimer's, catastrophic pulmonary aspiration, and multiple other issues had taken their toll. You once were a perfectly healthy, all-star basketball player and athletic physique, plus outward and inner beauty, now reduced to a mere shell of your former self. Once an artist without equal (1st prize at High Museum in Atlanta and

The Depression Pilgrim's Journey
The Man Who Walked through Time

numerous other regional juried competitions), you could no longer bless others with your matchless gift because of Parkinson's tremors. Totally committed Christian, Sunday School teacher, dedicated homemaker, spouse, mom, prayer partner and best friend, and counselor/comforter to legions of hurting children: always serving Christ, family, and others, you became totally dependent upon us who loved you.

While you struggled for more than a decade through your myriad impairments, with the help of others, I was honored in the home you made for us to give you 24/7 personal care, which you so richly deserved. Putting God, family, and others before self and then yourself last, you lovingly cared for all of us for decades, and it was my honor and privilege to care for you in your time of need. I was with you while you escaped this "prison of clay" in the early morning hours of July 15, 2017. You are now whole again and at peace. And, as one of your nine physicians said … "You beat me home!"

You are fondly remembered and sorely missed by the children and me and by all of the innumerable sojourners to whom you ministered and whose lives you "En-Ritched" while you were with us. Our assured promise is that we shall see you and be with you again. "For the Lord himself shall descend from heaven with a shout, with the voice of the archangel, and with the trump of God,

The Depression Pilgrim's Journey
The Man Who Walked through Time

and the dead in Christ shall rise first. Then we who are alive and remain shall be caught up together with them in the clouds, to meet the Lord in the air, and so shall we ever be with the Lord" (1 Thessalonians 4:16-17). This is our "blessed hope" (Titus 2:13).

Sorely missed by: Dr. Paul A. Ritch, Barbara, Sherman, Trena, Gary, Dennis, and caregivers Earlene Ward, Barbara Fairweather, Gwen Gott, Alexian Home Care, Home Instead, RN's, LPNs, CNAs, and numerous sitters.

See you soon, Sweetheart!

Paul

First anniversary of Joyce's homegoing.

Joyce Ann Ritch Memorial 2018.07.15

The Depression Pilgrim's Journey
The Man Who Walked through Time

Safe in the New Year

1. Avoid riding in automobiles. They are responsible for 20% of all fatal accidents.

2. Do not stay at home because 17% of all accidents occur in the home.

3. Avoid travel by air, rail, or water because 16% of all accidents involve these three.

4. Avoid walking on streets or sidewalks because 14% of all accidents occur to pedestrians.

5. Of the remaining 33%, 32% of all deaths occur in hospitals. AVOID hospitals!!

6. You might be amazed to learn that only .001% of deaths occur during worship services in church, and these are usually related to previous physical disorders. Therefore, logic tells us that the safest place on earth at any given time is at church!

And, finally, Bible study is safe too. Surprisingly, the percentage of deaths during Bible study is even less!

So, for your own safety's sake, attend church and read your Bible. It could save your life!

The Depression Pilgrim's Journey
The Man Who Walked through Time

End of Chapter

The Depression Pilgrim's Journey
The Man Who Walked through Time

Chapter 5
Collections of Humor
Communication Albert Mehrabian

COMMUNICATIONS

MESSAGE VIA HUMAN MEDIUM

CARRIER	% OF MESSAGE CARRIED
VERBAL (CONTENT)	7
VOCAL (CHARACTERISTICS)	38
FACIAL ACTIONS (NON-VERBAL)	55

****

NON-VERBAL (HUMAN ELEMENTS)
1. FACIAL EXPRESSIONS EYE CONTACT, ETC.
2. GESTURES, ACTIONS
3. POSTURE, POSITION
4. VOCAL CHARACTERISTICS

NON-VERBAL (NON-HUMAN ELEMENTS)
1. USE OF TIME (CONFERENCES, INSTRUCTION, EVALUATION)
2. USE OF SPACE (PRIVACY, TOGETHERNESS, ETC.)

The Depression Pilgrim's Journey
The Man Who Walked through Time

Often confusing English words

1. "Run" has indeed become the single word with the most potential meanings in all of English, boasting no fewer than 645 different usage cases for the verb form alone!

2. "Set" Even today, the print edition of the OED contains some 200 meanings for 'set', beginning with "put, lay, or stand (something) in a specified place or position," and continuing on for about 32 pages. If that doesn't intimidate you, find out how long it would take to read the entire dictionary.

3. "Strike" (Paul's observations) English is general at best; it draws much from many languages, and sometimes the same word has many meanings. Consider the word "strike", it could mean you're at a bowling alley, and all the pins are down; at a ballgame, and one more and you're out; when collective bargaining reached an impasse, and employees walked off the job; a bomber pilot and you're about to drop tons of 'advice' on the enemy; etc.

4. The Scottish have 421 words for "Snow"! (Reader's Digest).

5. The longest English word is 189,819 letters!

Pneumonoultramicroscopicsilicovolcanoconiosis, a type of lung disease. (Reader's Digest).

6. Etc. Ad Infinitum!

The Depression Pilgrim's Journey
The Man Who Walked through Time

Communication Problem

COMMUNICATION PROBLEM

I know you believe you understand what you think I said, but I am not sure you realize that what you heard is not what I meant.

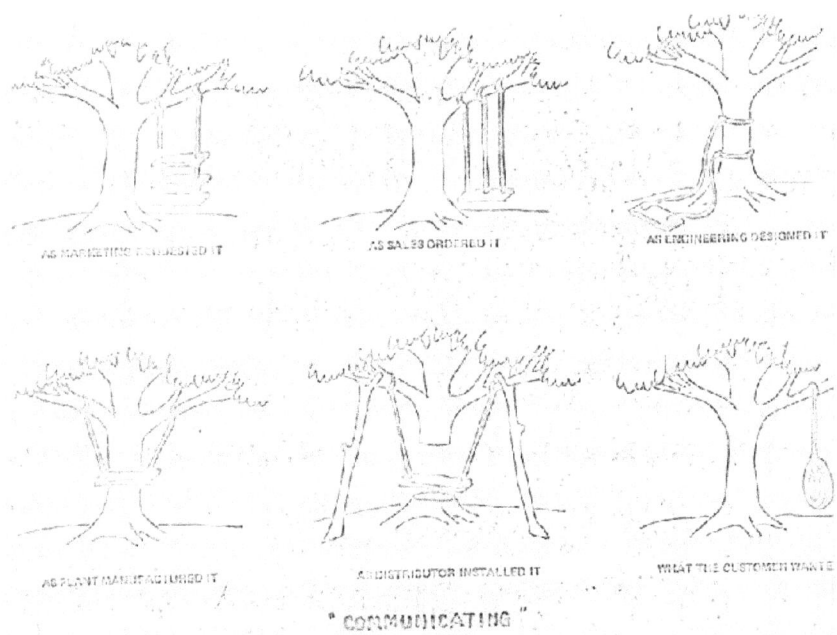

The Depression Pilgrim's Journey
The Man Who Walked through Time

<u>Examples Of Unclear Writing Sentences</u> Taken From Actual Letters Received By The Local Welfare Department In Appl. Applications For Support.

1. I am forwarding my marriage certificate and six children. I have seven but one died which was baptized on a half sheet of paper.

2. I am writing the Welfare Department to say that my baby was born three years ago. When do I get my money?

3. Mrs. Jones has not had any clothes for a year and has been visited regularly by the minister.

4. I cannot get sick pay. I have six children. Can you tell me why?

5. I am glad to report that my husband who is missing is dead.

6. This is my eighth child. What are you going to do about it?

7. Please find for certain if my husband is dead. The man I am now living with won't eat or do anything until he knows.

8. I am very much annoyed to find that you have branded my son illiterate. This is a dirty lie, as I was married a week before he was born.

9. In answer to your letter, I have given birth to a boy weighing 10 pounds. I hope this is satisfactory.

10. I am forwarding my marriage certificate and my three children. One of which is a mistake, as you can see.

11. My husband got his project cut off two weeks ago and I haven't had any relief since.

12. Unless I get my husband's money pretty soon, I will be forced to lead an immortal life.

13. You have changed my little boy to a girl. Will this makes a difference?

14. I have no children as yet as my husband is a truck driver and works day and night.

15. In accordance with your instructions, I have given birth to twins in the enclosed enveloped.

16. I want my money as quick as I can get it. I have been in bed with the doctor for 2 weeks and he doesn't do me any good. If things don't improve, I'll have to send for another doctor.

The Depression Pilgrim's Journey
The Man Who Walked through Time

Halleys Breakdown in Communication

A BREAKDOWN IN COMMUNICATIONS

It's been said that as much as 80 per cent of the meaning of any message can be lost as it is passed down through 3 or 4 levels of authority. We call it "Communications Breakdown." Here's a classic example:

"Operation Halley's Comet"

A Colonel issued the following directive to his Executive Officer:

"Tomorrow evening at approximately 2000 hours, Halley's Comet will be visible in this area, an event which occurs only once every 75 years. Have the men fall out in the battalion area in fatigues, and I will explain this rare phenomenon to them. In case of rain, we will not be able to see anything, so assemble the men in the theater, and I'll show them films of it."

The Executive Officer writes to the Company Commander:

"By order of the Colonel tomorrow at 2000 hours Halley's Comet will appear before the battalion area. If it rains, fall the men out in fatigues and march to the theater where the rare phenomenon will take place, something which occurs only once every 75 years."

The Company Commander to the Lieutenant:

"By order of the Colonel, in fatigues at 2000 hours tomorrow evening the phenomenal Halley's Comet will appear in the theater. In case of rain in the battalion area, the Colonel will give another order, something that occurs only once every 75 years."

Lieutenant to the Sergeant:

"Tomorrow at 2000 hours, the Colonel will appear in the theater with Halley's Comet, something that appears every 75 years. If it rains, the Colonel will order the comet into the battalion area."

The Sergeant to the Squad:

"When it rains tomorrow at 2000 hours the phenomenal 75 year old General Halley, accompanied by the Colonel, will drive his comet through the battalion area theater in his fatigues."

So there you have it a little breakdown in communications !

The Depression Pilgrim's Journey
The Man Who Walked through Time

Pilot who Speaks Blonde

A plane is on its way to Houston when
a blonde in economy class gets up and
moves to the first-class section and sits down.

The flight attendant watches her do this and
asks to see her ticket. She then tells the blonde
that she paid for economy class, and that she will
have to sit in the back. The blonde replies,
"I'm blonde, I'm beautiful, I'm going to Houston, and
I'm staying right here."

The flight attendant goes into the cockpit and
tells the pilot and the copilot that there is a
blonde bimbo sitting in first class that
belongs in the economy and won't move back to her seat

The copilot goes back to the blonde and tries to
explain that because she only paid for economy, she
will have to leave and return to her seat.
The blonde replies,
"I'm blonde, I'm beautiful, I'm going to Houston, and
I'm staying right here."

The Depression Pilgrim's Journey
The Man Who Walked through Time

The copilot tells the pilot that he probably should
have the police waiting when they land in Houston to
arrest this blonde woman who won't listen to reason.

The pilot says, "You say she is a blonde?
I'm married to a blonde, I speak blonde, let me talk to her."

He goes back to the blonde and whispers in her ear,
and she says, "Oh, thank you"; Gets up and immediately
goes back to her seat in economy

The flight attendant and copilot are amazed and
ask him what he said to make her move.
"I told her, first class isn't going to Houston!!"

The Depression Pilgrim's Journey
The Man Who Walked through Time

If, when you say "Whiskey" (Courtesy, Paul A. Ritch)

An old lawyer running for the state legislature in one of the last citadels of prohibition was put on the spot by the local newspaper editor, who demanded to know how he stood upon the question of whiskey. The old lawyer replied by saying, "Sir, you ask how I stand on the question of whiskey. I had not intended to discuss this controversial subject at this particular time, but I want you to know I am willing to discuss any subject at any time, regardless of how fraught with controversy it may be. Well, sir, here is my stand:

If when you say whiskey, you mean the devil's brew, the poison scourge, the bloody monster that defiles innocence, dethrones reason, creates misery and despair, yes, literally takes bread out of the mouths of babes...if you mean that vile drink which topples the Christian man and woman from pinnacles of gracious, righteous living into the bottomless pit of shame and despair, helplessness and hopelessness...then, sir, I am against it with every fiber in my body.

But if, when you say whiskey, you mean the oil of conversation, if you mean that philosophic drink which is consumed when good fellows get together, which puts a song in their hearts, laughter on their lips, and a smile of contentment in their eyes; if you mean Christmas cheer; if you mean that stimulating drink which puts the spring in an old man's step on a

The Depression Pilgrim's Journey
The Man Who Walked through Time

frosty morning; if you mean that drink which permits a man to magnify his joys and happiness and to forget (if only for a moment) life's tragedies and sorrows; if you mean that drink which pours into our treasury untold millions with which we provide tender care for our little crippled children, our aged and infirmed, and with which we build schools, hospitals, and roads...then, sir, I am for it with all my heart.

There, sir, is my stand. From it I shall not retract; I will not compromise. This is my final word on the subject."

The Depression Pilgrim's Journey
The Man Who Walked through Time

Grandmother Witness

In a trial, a Southern small-town prosecuting attorney called his first witness, a grandmotherly elderly woman, to the witness stand.

He approached her and asked, "Mrs. Jones, do you know me?"

She responded, "Why, yes, I do know you, Mr. Williams. I have known you since you were a young boy, and frankly, you have been a big disappointment to me. You lie, you cheat on your wife, and you manipulate people and talk about them behind their backs. You think you are a big shot when you haven't the brains to realize you never will amount to anything more than a two-bit paper pusher. Yes, I know you."

The lawyer was stunned! Not knowing what else to do, he pointed across the room and asked, "Mrs. Jones, do you know the defense attorney?"

She again replied, "Why yes, I do. I have known Mr. Bradley since he was a youngster, too. He's lazy, bigoted, and he has a drinking problem. He can't build a normal relationship with anyone, and his law practice is one of the worst in the entire state. Not to mention, he cheated on his wife with three different women. One of them was your wife. Yes, I know him."

The defense attorney almost died.

The Depression Pilgrim's Journey
The Man Who Walked through Time

The judge asked both counselors to approach the bench and, in a very quiet voice, said, "If either of you idiots asks her if she knows me, I'll send you to the electric chair."

The Depression Pilgrim's Journey
The Man Who Walked through Time

49 Actual Newspaper Headlines (collected by journalists)
Draw your conclusions

1. Something went wrong in the jet crash, expert says
2. Police begin campaign to run down Jaywalkers
3. Safety experts say school bus passengers should be belted
4. Drunk gets nine months in a violin case
5. Survivor of Siamese twins joins parents
6. Farmer bill dies in house
7. Iraqi head seeks arms
8. Lung cancer in women mushrooms
9. Eye drops off shelf
10. Teacher strikes idle kids
11. Clinton wins on budget, but more lies ahead
12. Squad helps dog bite victim
13. Shot off woman's leg helps Nicklaus to 66
14. Enraged cow injures farmer with axe
15. Plane Too Close to Ground, Crash Probe Told
16. Miners Refuse to Work after Death
17. Juvenile Court to Try Shooting Defendant
18. Stolen Painting Found by Tree
19. Two Soviet Ships Collide, One Dies
20. Two Sisters Reunited after 18 Years in Checkout Counter
21. Killer Sentenced to Die for Second Time in 10 Years
22. Drunken Drivers Paid $1000 in '84

The Depression Pilgrim's Journey
The Man Who Walked through Time

23. War Dims Hope for Peace

24. If Strike isn't Settled Quickly, It May Last a While

25. Cold Wave Linked to Temperatures

26. Enfields Couple Slain; Police Suspect Homicide

27. Red Tape Holds Up New Bridge

28. Deer Kill 17,000

29. Typhoon Rips Through Cemetery; Hundreds Dead

30. Man Struck by Lightning Faces Battery Charge

31. New Study of Obesity Looks for Larger Test Group

32. Astronaut Takes Blame for Gas in Spacecraft

33. Kids Make Nutritious Snacks

34. Chef Throws His Heart into Helping Feed Needy

35. Arson Suspect is Held in Massachusetts Fire

36. British Union Finds Dwarfs in Short Supply

37. Ban On Soliciting Dead in Trotwood

38. Lansing Residents Can Drop Off Trees

39. Local High School Dropouts Cut in Half

40. New Vaccine May Contain Rabies

41. Man Minus Ear Waives Hearing

42. Deaf College Opens Doors to Hearing

43. Air Head Fired

44. Steals Clock, Faces Time

45. Old School Pillars are Replaced by Alumni

The Depression Pilgrim's Journey
The Man Who Walked through Time

46. Bank Drive-In Window Blocked by Board

47. Hospitals are Sued by 7 Foot Doctors

48. Some Pieces of Rock Hudson Sold at Auction

49. Include your Children When Baking Cookies

The Depression Pilgrim's Journey
The Man Who Walked through Time

Church Bulletin Bloopers

The following have actually appeared in church bulletins!

- This afternoon, there will be a baptismal in the south and north ends of the church. Children will be baptized on both ends.
- Tuesday at 4 p.m., there will be an ice cream social. All ladies giving milk, please come early.
- Wednesday, the ladies literary society will meet. Mrs. Johnson will sing "Put me in my little bed" accompanied by the pastor.
- Thursday at 5 p.m., there will be a meeting of the Little Mothers Club. All wishing to become Little Mothers, please meet the minister in his study.
- This being Easter Sunday, we will ask Mrs. Johnson to come forward and lay an egg on the alter.
- The service will close with "Little Drops of Water"…one of the ladies will start quietly and the rest of the congregation will join in.
- This morning, a collection will be taken to defray the expense of the new carpet. All wishing to do something on the carpet, please come forward and get a piece of paper.

The Depression Pilgrim's Journey
The Man Who Walked through Time

- The ladies of the church have cast off clothing of every kind and they may be seen in the church basement on Friday afternoon.

- This evening at 7 p.m., there will be a hymn sing in the park across from the church. Bring a blanket and come prepared to sin.

The Depression Pilgrim's Journey
The Man Who Walked through Time
'SIGNS' of the Times

The following signs have been sighted:

On a septic tank truck: "Yesterday's meals on wheels."

On another septic tank truck: "We're #1 in the #2 business."

At a gynecologist's office: "Dr. Jones, at your cervix."

At a proctologist's office: "To expedite your visit, please back in."

On a plumber's truck: "We repair what your husband 'fixed'"

On another plumber's truck: "Don't sleep with a drip; call your plumber."

At a tire shop: "Invite us to your next blowout."

At a towing company: "We don't charge an arm & a leg ... we want tows."

On an electrician's truck: "Let us remove your shorts."

On a maternity room door: "Push, push, push."

At an optometrist's: "If you don't see what you're looking for, you're at the right place."

At a pizza shop: "Seven days without pizza makes one weak."

At a non-smoking area: "If we see smoke, we assume you're on fire and turn the hose on."

The Depression Pilgrim's Journey
The Man Who Walked through Time

On a taxidermist's window: "We really know our stuff."

On a homeowner's fence: "Salesmen welcome ...dog food is expensive."

At a podiatrist's office: "Time wounds all heels."

At a veterinarian's office: "Will be back in five minutes. Sit! Stay!"

At an electric company: "We would be de-lighted with your payment; if not, you will be."

At a restaurant: "Don't stand there hungry; come on in and get fed up."

At a muffler shop: "No appointment necessary ... we hear your coming."

At a car dealership: "Best way to get back on your feet ... miss a payment."

In front yard of a funeral home: "Drive carefully; we'll wait."

At a propane filling station: "Thank heaven for little grills."

At a Chicago radiator shop: "Best place in town to take a leak."

The Depression Pilgrim's Journey
The Man Who Walked through Time

Excerpts from the Hospital

Actual writings on hospital charts:

1. She has no rigors or shaking chills, but her husband states she was very hot in bed last night.
2. Patient has chest pain if she lies on her left side for over a year
3. On the second day, the knee was better, and on the third day, it disappeared.
4. The patient is tearful and crying constantly. She also appears to be depressed.
5. The patient has been depressed since she began seeing me in 1993.
6. Discharge status: alive but without my permission.
7. Healthy appearing decrepit 69-year-old male, mentally alert but forgetful.
8. The patient refused autopsy.
9. The patient has no previous history of suicides.
10. Patient has left white blood cells at another hospital.
11. Patient's medical history has been remarkably insignificant, with only a 40-pound weight gain in the past three days.
12. Patient had waffles for breakfast and anorexia for lunch.
13. She is numb from her toes down.
14. While in ER, she was examined, x-rated, and sent home.

The Depression Pilgrim's Journey
The Man Who Walked through Time

15. The skin was moist and dry.
16. Occasional, constant, infrequent headaches.
17. Patient was alert and unresponsive.
18. Rectal examination revealed a normal-sized thyroid.
19. She stated that she had been constipated for most of her life until she got a divorce.
20. I saw your patient today, who is still under our care for physical therapy.
21. Both breasts are equal and reactive to light and accommodation.
22. Examination of genitalia reveals that he is circus-sized.
23. The lab test indicated abnormal lower function.
24. The patient was to have a bowel resection. However, he took a job as a stockbroker instead.
25. Skin: somewhat pale but present
26. The pelvic exam will be done later on the floor
27. Patient was seen in consultation by Dr. Blank, who felt we should sit on the abdomen, and I agree.
28. Large brown stool ambulating in the hall.
29. Patient has two teenage children, but no other abnormalities.

The Depression Pilgrim's Journey
The Man Who Walked through Time

A Few of Life's Little 'Mysteries'

- Why does the sun lighten our hair and darken our skin?
- Why can't women put on mascara with their mouth closed?
- Why doesn't glue stick to the inside of the bottle?
- Why do we never see a headline: "Psychic Wins Lottery"?
- Why is 'abbreviated' such a 'long' word?
- Why is a boxing 'ring' square?
- Why is it called 'lipstick' when you can still move your lips?
- Why do doctors call what they do 'practice'?
- Why is it that rain 'drops' and snow 'falls'?
- Why, when driving and looking for an address,... you turn down the volume on the radio?
- Why is bottled lemon juice made with 'artificial' flavor ... and dishwashing liquid made with 'real' lemons?
- Why is the man who invests your money called ... a 'broker'?
- Why is the third hand on your watch called ... a 'second' hand?
- Why is the slowest traffic of the day called ... 'rush' hour?
- Why is the word 'dictionary' in the dictionary?
- Why isn't there a 'mouse-flavored' cat food?
- Why don't they make the whole airplane out of that stuff they make the 'indestructible' little black box?

The Depression Pilgrim's Journey
The Man Who Walked through Time

- How is it that 'fat' people can go 'skinny-dipping'?
- Why do you need a driver's license to buy liquor ... and yet you can't drink and drive?
- Why are 'green' blackberries 'red'?
- How do you put a 'square meal' in a 'round' stomach?
- Why does the same sun 'melt' butter and 'bake' bricks?
- Why is the shortest sentence 'I am' ... and the longest I do'???
- Why do you never learn to swear until you learn to drive?
- Why do we drive on a 'parkway' ... and park on a 'driveway'?
- Why is 'overlook' and 'oversee' different things?
- If four out of five people 'suffer' from diarrhea ... does that mean that the fifth one 'enjoys' it?
- Why are croutons in airtight packages ..., aren't they just stale bread anyway?
- When something is malfunctioning ... it is 'out of whack'. What's a 'whack'?
- Do infants enjoy infancy as much as adults do adultery?
- If we truly are here to help others ... what are they here for?
- When offered 'a penny for your thoughts' ... you put in your 'two cents'. What happens to the other penny?
- If love is so blind ... why is lingerie so popular?

The Depression Pilgrim's Journey
The Man Who Walked through Time

- How is it that a black cow can eat 'green' grass, give 'white' milk and 'yellow' butter, and then that grow 'red' hair on a kid's head???

The Depression Pilgrim's Journey
The Man Who Walked through Time

Holy Humor

Holy humor

The choir is ready to sing and here are some suggested hymns, compliments of Becky Witt at the Hamilton County Baptist Association.

The dentist's hymn: *Crown Him With Many Crowns.*

The TV weatherman's hymn: *There Shall Be Showers of Blessing.*

The contractor's hymn: *The Church's One Foundation.*

The tailor's hymn: *Holy, Holy, Holy.*

The golfer's hymn: *There Is a Green Hill Far Away.*

The politician's hymn: *Standing on the Promises.*

The optometrist's hymn: *Open Mine Eyes That I Might See.*

The IRS hymn: *All to Thee.*

The gossiper's hymn: *Pass It On.*

The electrician's hymn: *Send the Light.*

The shopper's hymn: *Sweet By and By.*

The Depression Pilgrim's Journey
The Man Who Walked through Time

Humor Stupidity
Spread and make someone smile today!

Only in This Stupid World

Do drugstores make the sick walk all the way to the back of the store to get their prescriptions, while healthy people can buy cigarettes at the front.

Only in This Stupid World

Do people order double cheeseburgers, large fries, and a "DIET" Coke.

Only in This Stupid World

Do banks leave vault doors open and then chain the pens to the counters.

Only in This Stupid World

Do we leave cars worth thousands of dollars in the driveway and put our useless junk in the garage.

Only in This Stupid World

do we buy hot dogs in packages of twelve and buns in Packages of eight.

EVER WONDER:

The Depression Pilgrim's Journey
The Man Who Walked through Time

Why the sun lightens our hair, but darkens our skin?

Why is 'abbreviated' such a long word?

Why is it that doctors call what they do 'practice'?

Why is lemon juice made with artificial flavor, and dishwashing liquid made with real lemons?

Why is the man who invests all your money called a broker?

Why is the time of day with the slowest traffic called rush hour?

Why isn't there mouse-flavored cat food?

Why didn't Noah swat those two mosquitoes?

Why do they sterilize the needle for lethal injections?

You know that indestructible black box that is used on airplanes? Why don't they make the whole plane out of that stuff?!

Why don't sheep shrink when it rains? (Wool??)

Why are they called apartments, when they are all stuck together?

If con is the opposite of pro, is Congress the opposite of progress?

If flying is so safe, why do they call the airport the terminal?

The Depression Pilgrim's Journey
The Man Who Walked through Time

Now that you've smiled at least once, it's your turn to spread the stupidity and send this to someone to which you want to bring a smile.

Borrowed and "En-Ritched" by Paul A. Ritch

The Depression Pilgrim's Journey
The Man Who Walked through Time

Perspective

Situation: Susie goes off to College

Susie does not write home as she should

Susie plays & does not study

Grade report time

What to do? What to do?

"Dear Mother and Dad:

Since I left for college, I have been remiss in writing, and I am sorry for my thoughtlessness in not having written before. I will bring you up to date now, but before you read on, please sit down. You are not to read any further unless you are sitting down. Okay?

Well, then, I am getting along pretty well now. The skull fracture and the concussion I got when I jumped out of the window of my dormitory when it caught on fire shortly after my arrival here is pretty well healed now. I only spent two weeks in the hospital, and now I can see almost normally and only get those sick headaches once a day. Fortunately, the fire in the dormitory and my jump was witnessed by an attendant at the gas station near the dorm, and he was the one who called the Fire Department and the ambulance. He also visited me in the hospital, and since I had nowhere to live because of the burnt-out dormitory, he was kind enough to invite me to share his apartment with him. It's really a basement room, but it's kind of cute. He is a very fine boy, and we

The Depression Pilgrim's Journey
The Man Who Walked through Time

have fallen deeply in love and are planning to get married. We haven't got the exact date yet, but it will be before my pregnancy begins to show.

Yes, Mother and Dad, I am pregnant. I know how much you are looking forward to being grandparents, and I know you will welcome the baby and give it the same love and devotion and tender care you gave me when I was a child. The reason for the delay in our marriage is that my boyfriend has a minor infection, which prevents us from passing our pre-marital blood tests, and I carelessly caught it from him.

I know that you will welcome him into our family with open arms. He is kind and, although not well educated, he is ambitious. Although he is of a different race and religion than ours, I know your often-expressed tolerance will not permit you to be bothered by that.

Now that I have brought you up to date, I want to tell you that there was no dormitory fire, I did not have a concussion or skull fracture, I was not in the hospital, I am not pregnant, I am not engaged, I am not infected, and there is no boyfriend in my life. However, I am getting a D in History and an F in Science, and I want you to see those marks in their proper perspective.

Your loving daughter, Susie."

The Depression Pilgrim's Journey
The Man Who Walked through Time

The Barometer Story
A Problem in Stating Desired Behavior and Accurately Measuring that Behavior

By Dr. Alexander Calandra

Washington University, St. Louis

Some time ago, I received a call from a colleague who asked if I would be the referee on the grading of an examination question. It seemed that he was about to give a student a zero for 4is answer to a physics question, while the student claimed he should receive a perfect score and would do so if the system were not set up against the student. The instructor and the student agreed to submit this to an impartial arbiter, and I was selected.

The Barometer Problem

I went to my colleague's office and read the examination question, which was "show how it is possible to determine the height of a tall building with the aid of a barometer."

The student's answer was, "Take the barometer to the top of the building, attach a long rope to it, lower the barometer to the street, then bring it up, measuring the length of the rope. The length of the rope is the height of the building."

Now, this is a very interesting answer, but should the student get credit for it? I pointed out that the student really had a strong

The Depression Pilgrim's Journey
The Man Who Walked through Time

case for full credit, since he had answered the question completely and correctly. On the other hand, if full credit were given, it could well contribute to a high grade for the student in his physics course. A high grade is supposed to certify that the student knows some physics, but the answer to the question did not confirm this. With this in mind, I suggested that the student have another try at answering the question. I was not surprised that my colleague agreed to this, but I was surprised that the student did. Acting in terms of the agreement, I gave the student six minutes to answer the question, with the warning that the answer should show some knowledge of physics. I asked if he wished to give up, since I had another class to take care of, but he said no, he was not giving up. He had many answers to this problem, and he was just thinking of the best one. I excused myself for interrupting him and asked him to please go on. In the next minute, he dashed off his answer, which was:

"Take the barometer to the top of the building and lean over the edge of the roof. Drop the barometer, timing its fall with a stopwatch. Then, using the formula S t 1/2 Hz, calculate the height of the building."

At this point, I asked my colleague if he would give up. He conceded, and I gave the student almost full credit. In leaving my

The Depression Pilgrim's Journey
The Man Who Walked through Time

colleague's office, I recalled that the student had said he had other answers to the problem, so I asked him what they were.

"Oh, yes," said the student. "There are many ways of getting the height of a tall building with the aid of a barometer. For example, you could take the barometer out on a sunny day and measure the height of the barometer, the length of its shadow, and the length of the shadow of the building, and by the use of simple proportion, determine the height of the building."

"Fine," I said. "And the others?"

"Yes," said the student. "There is a very basic measurement method that you will like. In this method, you take the barometer and begin to walk up the stairs. As you climb the stairs, you mark off the length, and this will give you the height of the building in barometer units. A very direct method."

"Of course, if you want a more sophisticated method, you can tie the barometer to the end of a string, swing it as a pendulum. And determine the value of 'g' at the street level and at the top of the building. From the difference between the two values of 'g', the height of the building can, in principle, be calculated?"

Finally, he concluded, "If you don't limit me to physics solutions to this problem, there are many other answers, such as taking the barometer to the basement and knocking on the

The Depression Pilgrim's Journey
The Man Who Walked through Time

superintendent's door. When the superintendent answers, you speak to him as follows: 'Dear Mr. Superintendent, here I have a very fine barometer. If you tell me the height of this building, I will give you this barometer!'"

At this point, I asked the student if he really didn't know the answer to the problem. He admitted that he did, but that he was so fed up with college instructors trying to teach him how to think and to use critical thinking, instead of showing him the structure of the subject matter, he decided to take off on what he regarded mostly as a sham.

The Depression Pilgrim's Journey
The Man Who Walked through Time

Don't Let Go of the Rope!

I am writing in response to your request for additional information. In block # 3 of the accident reporting form, I put "Poor Planning" as the cause of my accident. You said in your letter that I should EXPLAIN MORE FULLY, and I trust that the following details will be sufficient.

I am a bricklayer by trade. On the day of the accident, I was working alone on the roof of a six-story building. When I completed my work, I discovered that I had about 500 pounds of brick left over. Rather than carry the bricks down by hand, I decided to lower them down in a barrel by using a pulley, which, fortunately, was attached to the side of the building on the sixth floor.

Securing the rope at ground level, I went to the roof, swung the barrel out, and loaded the brick into it. Then I went back to the ground and untied the rope, holding it tightly to secure a slow descent of the 500 pounds of bricks. You will note in block # 11 of the accident reporting form that I weigh 135.

Due to my surprise at being jerked off the ground so suddenly, I lost my presence of mind and forgot to let go of the rope. Needless to say, I proceeded at a rather rapid rate up the side of the building.

The Depression Pilgrim's Journey
The Man Who Walked through Time

In the vicinity of the third floor, I met the barrel coming down. This will explain the fractured skull and broken collarbone.

Slowed only slightly, I continued my rapid ascent, not stopping until the fingers of my right hand were two knuckles deep into the pulley. Fortunately, by this time, I had regained my presence of mind and was able to hold on tightly to the rope... in spite of my pain.

At approximately the same time, however, the barrel of bricks hit the ground, and the bottom fell out of the barrel. Devoid of the weight of the bricks, the barrel weighed approximately 50 pounds.

I refer you again to my weight as specified in block # 11. As you can imagine, I began a rapid descent down the side of the building.

In the vicinity of the third floor, I again encountered the barrel coming up: This accounts for the two fractured ankles and the laceration of my legs and lower body.

The encounter with the barrel slowed me enough to lessen my injuries when I fell on the pile of bricks, and, fortunately, only three (3) vertebrae were cracked.

1 am sorry to report, however, that as I lay on the bricks in pain and unable to stand, and watching the empty barrel six stories

The Depression Pilgrim's Journey
The Man Who Walked through Time

above, I again lost my presence of mind ... and I LET GO OF THE ROPE!!!

The Depression Pilgrim's Journey
The Man Who Walked through Time

If Jesus Came Today

If Jesus came today to do His same ministry on earth as He did in the 1st century ... He would be in trouble:

- With the Food and Drug Administration (FDA)
  for turning water into wine without a license
- With the Environmental Protection Agency (EPA)
  for killing fig trees
- With the American Medical Association (AMA)
  for practicing medicine without a license
- With the Department of Health
  for feeding 5,000 people in the wilderness
  for asking people to open graves
  for raising the dead
- With the National Education Association (NEA)
  for teaching without a license
- With the Occupational Safety & Health Administration (OSHA)
  for walking on water without a life jacket
- With the Society for the Prevention of Cruelty to Animals (SPCA)
  for driving hogs into the sea

The Depression Pilgrim's Journey
The Man Who Walked through Time

- With the national board of Psychiatrists
  for giving advice on how to live a guilt-free life
- With the National Organization of Women (NOW)
  for not choosing a female apostle
- With the Inter-Faith-Movement
  for condemning all other religions
- With the Abortion Rights League
  for saying that whoever harms children, it were better that they had not been born
- With the Zoning Department
  for building mansions without a permit!

Borrowed From: The Jacksonville Church of Christ
  329 Nisbet Street NW (Hwy 204)
  P. O. box 520
  Jacksonville, Alabama 36265

'En-Ritched': Paul A. Ritch
  Chattanooga TN 37421

The Depression Pilgrim's Journey
The Man Who Walked through Time
Paul's Occupation List

- Real Estate Purchaser .... U. R. Kidding
- Naturalist .... Ilene Dover
- Gardener........................... Ima Rose Budd
- Naval Officer...................... Archie Peligro
- Ophthalmologist.................... Seymour Freely
- Optometrist........................ I. C. Moore
- Southern Public Relations Agent.... Georgia Onmamind
- Highway Patrolman.................. U. R. Speeding
- Lumberjack......................... Buzz Sawyer
- Brick Layer........................ Mort R. Meeks
- Banker............................. Ima Teller
- Cosmetologist/Barber............... Fonda Haire
- Grump.............................. Ira Tate
- Female Inmate...................... Miss D. Meanor
- Florist............................ Violet Flowers
- Pharmacist......................... Vita Mynn
- Banker............................. Linda U. Dollar
- Pilot.............................. Rex Weekly

The Depression Pilgrim's Journey
The Man Who Walked through Time

- Urologist.......................... I. P. Daily
- Xray Technologist................... C. M. Bonz
- Teamster........................... I. R. Driver
- Podiatrist......................... Dr. Foote
- Ornithologist...................... Ben A. Byrd
- Nurse.............................. Kathy Riser
- Skin Flint......................... E. Connie Mizer
- Attorney........................... Sue M. Peeples
- Pasadena Florist................... Rose Bolles
- Mortician.......................... Paul Barrows
- Hermaphrodite...................... Newt R. Gender
- Meteorologist...................... Howell D. Weatherbee

By Paul A. Ritch

The Depression Pilgrim's Journey
The Man Who Walked through Time

Paulisms (2025)

1. The first baseball game ... In the "Big-inning" Genesis 1:1.

2. The first "Basket Case" ... Moses' Mom "put the child therein; and she laid it in the flags by the river's brink" Exodus 2:2-3.

3. The first known cigarette ... When Rebecca saw Isaac, she "lighted off the camel" Genesis 24:64.

4. The car that brought down the walls of Jericho ... "long blast with a Ram's horn" Jos.6:5.

5. Nebuchadnezzar drove a Plymouth ... "Then Nebuchadnezzar, in his rage and 'Fury' commanded to bring ..." Dan 3:13.
The Apostles drove a Honda ... "They were all in one Accord" Acts 2:1.

6. "Jesus said unto him (Peter), verily I say unto thee, that this night, before the cock crows, thou shalt deny me thrice" Mt 26:34. Peter "Chickened out".

7. Like the Pharisees, we "whitewash the pump hoping to purify the water" Mt.23:25,27

8. Moses was the O.T. "Basket Case" Ex. 2:2-3. Paul the apostle was the N.T. "Basket Case" Acts 9:24-25.

The Depression Pilgrim's Journey
The Man Who Walked through Time

9. Daniel spent a night in the "Lion's Den Hotel" Dan. 6:12-22 (The lions got "Lock Jaw" Dan. 6:22).

10. Jonah graduated from "Whale University" Jonah 1:17.

11. Achan got a "Wedgie" Joshua 7:24-26.

12. Wrestling an angel, Jacob got "All out of Joint" Gen: 32:24-25.

13. Joseph was: Pampered in Papa's house Gen.37:3; Prisoned in Potiphar's House Gen.39:20; and, Promoted in Pharoah's house Gen.41:41.

14. My Church was full of willing workers … 5 willing to work, all others willing to let them!

15. The Titanic built by professionals …. the Ark by an amateur!

16. The snails were on board the Ark with the Cheetahs!

17. Demons of Gadara cast into swine who drowned Luke 8:33 They committed "Suey-Cide"!

18. "Time Stands Still", vs "A Face That Would Stop a Clock".

19. God won't look you over for medals & honors but for battle scars!

The Depression Pilgrim's Journey
The Man Who Walked through Time

20. I found out I can't take it with me, so I'm sending it in advance! (Billy Graham observed, "Never saw a U-Haul following a hearse"!

21. "He is no fool who gives up what he cannot keep to gain that which he cannot lose". NOT Jim Elliot, who claimed it in 1949, but Paul E. Holdcraft #232 in a booklet published in 1929!

22. You are called to be a witness … not a judge!

23. Rev.13:17-18, "Mark of the Beast". Gal.6:17, "Mark of the BEST"!

24. Live so even the undertaker is sad! Borrowed from Mark Twain.

25. God doesn't call the "Qualified". He qualifies the "Called" 1 Cor. 1:27-30.

26. Algebra is about equations. "Trigger-Nometry" is about a gun.

27. "Z-Bra" is the largest size you can buy.

28. College degrees, honors, accolades, etc., are like a curl on a pig's tail … doesn't add much value … just a little dignity!

29. Having a hard time? Do not dream, drift, and drive. Man up!

The Depression Pilgrim's Journey
The Man Who Walked through Time

30. Reputation is what men think of you. Character is what God knows! What are you in the dark? Borrowed. Source unknown.

31. Wise men seeking Jesus were southern firemen ……… "They came from 'afar'".

32. God uses busy men … not busybodies.

33. Sin will keep you from the Bible. The Bible will keep you from sin.

34. The "Tater" family: "Dick-Tater", "Aggie-Tater", "Spec-Tater", "Emmi-Tater", "Hessie-Tater".

35. We use WD40 & Duct tape. God used nails!

36. Split-second, the time when light changes until the car behind honks.

37. Roe vs. Wade. Washington's decision at the Potomac.

38. David chose 5 smooth stones. He heard Goliath had 4 brothers. He was going after the whole family!

39. Constitutional right for short sleeves … right to bear (bare) arms.

40. You can count the seeds in an apple, but NOT the apples in a seed!

The Depression Pilgrim's Journey
The Man Who Walked through Time

41. In death, the pupils of the eye close last. They "Die-Late"! (Courtesy, Paul's Friend Dr. Cornelius Mance)

42. God's 2 Angel Protectors … "Goodness" & "Mercy" (Psa. 23:6.)

43. Engagement ring: a tournament put on a female finger to stop circulation!

44. Shortest Bible verse: "Jesus wept". Man's longest sentence: "I do!

The Depression Pilgrim's Journey
The Man Who Walked through Time

Paul's Tests Administered During His Career

- Otis Quick Scoring
- Culture Fair Test
- Personality Inventory
- McQuaid Occupational
- Concept Mastery
- MMPI
- SRA Kuder Preference Tests
- Vocational Test
- Personality Test
- Reading Test
- Frederick Emotional Test
- 16 P.F. (Attitudes & Interests)
- IBM Aptitude Tests
- Time Appreciation Test
- Word Appreciation Test
- Sentence Completion Test

The Depression Pilgrim's Journey
The Man Who Walked through Time

- Et al

And, I helped the Educational Testing Service in Developing Standardized CLEP tests & others.

Tests Administered by Paul

The Depression Pilgrim's Journey
The Man Who Walked through Time

Square Test of Logic

This is an exercise to test your logic

1	2	3	4
5	6	7	8
9	10	11	12
13	14	15	16

How many squares can you find?

The Depression Pilgrim's Journey
The Man Who Walked through Time

Wrong Thing to Say

A married couple was sitting in a fine restaurant when the wife looked over at a nearby table and saw a man in a drunken stupor.

The husband asked, "I notice you've been watching that man for some time now. Do you know him"?

"Yes," she replied. "He is my ex-husband and has been drinking like that ever since I left him four years ago."

"That's remarkable," the husband replied. "I wouldn't think anybody could celebrate that long."

Services Saturday 2:30 p.m. at Forever Green Mortuary.

The Depression Pilgrim's Journey
The Man Who Walked through Time

End of Chapter

Chapter 6
Closing Thoughts
Why I Believe the Bible to be the Word of God

I. **It's Amazing Composition**

A. Human writers had little in common; many did not know each other and were spread across timelines, never crossing paths, so there could be no collusion

1. Moses wrote in a desert

2. Joshua was a military general

3. Nehemiah was a royal cupbearer

4. Daniel was a prime minister in successive empires

5. Amos was a herdsman and gatherer of sycamore fruit

6. Luke was a physician

7. Peter, James, and John were lowly fishermen

8. Saul was a murderer turned Paul the Apostle

B. There was no uniformity of conditions or environment

1. Moses wrote in a desert

2. Paul wrote in a prison

3. John wrote from a remote island of Patmos

4. Others wrote from myriad and unlikely locations

The Depression Pilgrim's Journey
The Man Who Walked through Time

II.   Its Unique Completeness

A.   Says so much in a small space

1.   Creation of the universe in a few words (Gen.1)

2.   Elijah on Carmel (1Kgs. 18:36-37) 63 words

3.   Prayer of Jabez 1 (Chron 4:10) 33 words.

B.   Covers the origin, the purpose, and the destiny of man!

Re: Westminster Catechism question one and Eccl. 12:13

C.   No vital topic in the human condition is excluded.

III.   Its Unparalleled Teachings

A.   The Sermon on the Mount: the highest code of ethics

B.   The Twenty-Third Psalm: the highest balm for the soul

IV.   Its Scientific Accuracy

A.   In Anthropology and the very elements of the Human Body

B.   In Medicine and the "the life of the flesh is in the blood" (Lev. 17:11). Moses knew hundreds of years earlier!!

C.   In the Sphere of the Earth (Isaiah. 40:22); at that time most believed it flat

D.   In Egypt and Hebrew's Sojourn there; the Exodus; and the ruins of Jericho and others authenticate.

The Depression Pilgrim's Journey
The Man Who Walked through Time

E.   In the "treasures of the snow" (Job 38:22); then re: packing TNT in ice in WWII to avoid spontaneous explosion. Job already knew!

V.   Its Fulfilled Prophecy (Against "Chance Fulfillment").

A.   Statistical probability would nullify "chance"

(Among other subjects, I taught college statistics)

B.   Peter Stoner, professor emeritus of science at Westmont College, gave this illustration. "Imagine covering the entire state of Texas with silver dollars to a level of two feet deep. The number of silver dollars to cover the whole state of Texas would be 10 to the 17th power. Now, choose ONE silver dollar; mark it; and, drop it from an airplane. Thoroughly stir all the silver dollars over the whole state. Then, blindfold one man; tell him he can travel wherever he wishes in the state of Texas and somewhere along the way stop, reach down into the two feet of silver dollars, and pull up the specifically marked dollar. What do you think are the chances of his finding that one silver dollar?

Well, the chance of his finding that one silver dollar is the same as the chance the prophets had (10 to the 17th power) of only EIGHT of their prophecies being fulfilled in any one man in the future."

The Depression Pilgrim's Journey
The Man Who Walked through Time

Yet, ALL of the myriad prophecies about Jesus were fulfilled to the very letter, and, 16 were fulfilled in His last week of life!!

VI.　Its Amazing Preservation Though the ages

VII.　Its Transforming Power

A.　Early Church fathers faced martyrdom with dynamic power.

B.　Saul of Tarsus to Paul who 'turned the world upside down'

C.　Millions of believers are evidence of its power.

D.　This writer's own personal life-changing experience!

VIII.　It is Easier to Believe Than it is to Doubt

A.　We acknowledge wind, though we cannot see it.

B.　We acknowledge pain, though we do not see it.

C.　We acknowledge odor, though we do not see it.

D.　We acknowledge love, though we do not see it.

E.　We acknowledge an untold number of abstracts without seeing them, yet strain at the authority of the Bible.

F.　Why not accept the message of the following:

1.　Psalm 19 "the heavens declare the glory of God …"

2.　Psalm 8:3 the heavens "the work of God's fingers"

The Depression Pilgrim's Journey
The Man Who Walked through Time

3. Romans 1:20 "For the invisible things of him from the creation of the world are clearly seen, being understood by the things that are made, even His eternal power and Godhead; so that they are without excuse".

G. See "DESIGN" in ALL of the cosmos. Re:

1. The human body (the eye, etc.).

2. In the feather, leaves on a tree, et al.

3. See outline "God's wonders and miracles".

4. Et al.

H. The precision of the universe with one billion trillion stars in the known universe as of Fall 2021!

Psa. 147:4 "He tells the number of stars; He calls them all by name"! WOW!

Borrowed from various sources, Gideons, Billy Sunday, others, compiled and "En-Ritched."

The Depression Pilgrim's Journey
The Man Who Walked through Time

God's Wonders and Miracles

1.   The hatching of eggs

a.   Potato bug .... 7 days

b.   Canary .... 14 days

c.   Barnyard hen .... 21 days

d.   Ducks/geese .... 28 days

e.   Mallard .... 35 days

f.   Parrot & ostrich .... 42 days

NOTICE: ALL divisible by 7 (Number of days in a week)!

2.   Making of the elephant:

a.   4 legs bend forward in the same direction

b.   With this huge beast, God gave 4 fulcrums to arise from the ground easily!

3.   Making of the camel

4.   Making of the horse: rises from the ground on two front legs first.

5.   Making of the cow: rises from the ground on two hind legs first.

6.   Sections, Segments, and number of grains in nature

a.   Watermelon: even number of stripes on the rind

b.   Orange: even number of segments

c.   Ear of corn: even number of rows

d.   Stalk of wheat: even number of grains

The Depression Pilgrim's Journey
The Man Who Walked through Time

NOTICE: ALL grains in even numbers on the stalk!

e. Bunch of bananas:

i. Lowest row, an even number bananas

ii. Each row decreases by 1 (1 row, even; next row, odd number)!

7. Waves of the sea: …….26 to the minute in ALL weather!

8. Flowers to bloom at specified times

The Depression Pilgrim's Journey
The Man Who Walked through Time

The Amazing Camel and its Creator

In all my years, I have never learned about the Camel, and I especially enjoyed how it was presented.

If you ever doubted that God exists,
Meet the Very Technical, Highly Engineered
Dromedary Camel.

When I'm hungry, I'll eat almost anything-
A leather bridle, a piece of rope, my master's tent,
Or a pair of shoes.

The Depression Pilgrim's Journey
The Man Who Walked through Time

My mouth is so tough a thorny cactus doesn't bother it.

I love to chow down grass and other plants

That grows here in the Arabian desert

I'm a dromedary camel, the one-hump kind

That lives in hot deserts in the Middle East.

My hump, all eighty pounds of it,

Is filled with fat, my body fuel, not water, as some people believe.

My Mighty Maker gave it to me because

He knew I wouldn't always be able to find food.

As I travel across the hot sands.

When I don't find any chow, my body automatically

Takes fat from the hump, feeds my system,

And keeps me going strong.

This is my emergency food supply.

The Depression Pilgrim's Journey
The Man Who Walked through Time

If I can't find any plants to munch, my body uses up my hump.
When the hump gets smaller, it starts to tip to one side.
But when I get to a nice oasis and begin to eat again,
My hump soon builds back to normal.

I've been known to drink twenty-seven gallons of water in ten minutes.
My Master Designer made me in such a fantastic way that
In a matter of minutes, all the water I've swallowed
Travels to the billions of microscopic cells that make up my flesh.

The Depression Pilgrim's Journey
The Man Who Walked through Time

Naturally, the water I swallow first goes into my stomach.
There, thirsty blood vessels absorb and carry it to every part of my body.
Scientists have tested my stomach and found it empty.
Ten minutes after I've drunk twenty gallons.

In an eight-hour day, I can carry a four-hundred-pound load
A hundred miles across a hot, dry desert
And not stop once for a drink or something to eat.
In fact, I've been known to go eight days without a drink,
But then I look like a wreck.
I lose 227 pounds, my ribs show through my skin,
And I look terribly skinny.
But I feel great!
I look thin because the billions of cells lose their water.
They're no longer fat. They're flat.

The Depression Pilgrim's Journey
The Man Who Walked through Time

Normally, my blood contains 94 percent water, just like yours.
But when I can't find any water to drink,
The heat of the sun gradually robs a little water out of my blood.
Scientists have found that my blood can lose up to
40 percent of its water, and I'm still healthy.

Doctors say human blood has to stay very close to 94 percent water.
If you lose 5 percent of it, you can't see anymore; 10 percent, you can't
Hear, and you go insane; 12 percent, your blood is as thick as molasses
And your heart can't pump the thick stuff. It stops, and you're dead.

The Depression Pilgrim's Journey
The Man Who Walked through Time

But that's not true with me.

Why?

Scientists say my blood is different.

My red cells are elongated. Yours are round.

Maybe that's what makes the difference.

This proves I'm designed for the desert,

Or the desert is designed for me.

Did you ever hear of a design without a Designer?

After I find a water hole,

I'll drink for about ten minutes

And my skinny body starts to change almost immediately.

In that short time, my body fills out nicely, I don't look skinny

The Depression Pilgrim's Journey
The Man Who Walked through Time

anymore,

And I gain back the 227 pounds I lost.

Even though I lose a lot of water on the desert,

My body conserves it too.

Way in the beginning, when my intelligent Engineer made me,

He gave me a specially designed nose that saves water.

When I exhale, I don't lose much.

My nose traps that warm, moist air from my lungs.

And absorbs it in my nasal membranes.

Tiny blood vessels in those membranes take that back into my blood.

The Depression Pilgrim's Journey
The Man Who Walked through Time

How's that for a recycling system? Pretty cool, isn't it.

It works because my nose is cool.

My cool nose changes that warm moisture in the air

From my lungs into water.

But how does my nose get cool?

I breath in hot dry desert air,

And it goes through my wet nasal passages.

This produces a cooling effect, and my nose stays as much as

18 degrees cooler than the rest of my body.

I love to travel to the beautiful sand dunes.

It's really quite easy, because

My Creator gave me specially engineered sand shoes for feet.

My hooves are wide, and they get even wider when I step on them.

Each foot has two long, bony toes with tough, leathery skin between my soles, are a little like webbed feet.

The Depression Pilgrim's Journey
The Man Who Walked through Time

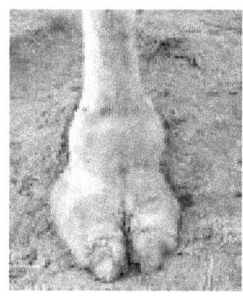

They won't let me sink into the soft, drifting sand.
This is good, because often my master wants me to carry him one hundred miles across the desert in just one day.
(I troop about ten miles per hour.)

Sometimes, a big windstorm comes out of nowhere, bringing flying sand with it.
My Master Designer put special muscles in my nostrils that close the openings, keeping sand out of my nose but still allowing me enough air to breathe.

The Depression Pilgrim's Journey
The Man Who Walked through Time

My eyelashes arch down over my eyes like screens,

keeping the sand and sun out, but still letting me see clearly.

If a grain of sand slips through and gets in my eye,

the Creator took care of that too.

He gave me an inner eyelid that automatically.

Wipes the sand off my eyeball just like a windshield wiper.

Some people think I'm conceited because I always walk around

with my head held high and my nose in the air.

But that's just because of the way I'm made.

My eyebrows are so thick and bushy

I have to hold my head high to peek out from underneath them.

The Depression Pilgrim's Journey
The Man Who Walked through Time

I'm glad I have them, though.
They shade my eyes from the bright sun.

Desert people depend on me for many things.
Not only am I their best form of transportation,
but I'm also their grocery store.
Mrs. Camel gives very rich milk
that people make into butter and cheese.
I shed my thick fur coat once a year,
and that can be woven into cloth.
A few young camels are used for beef,
but I don't like to talk about that.

For a long time we camels have been called
the "ships of the desert" because of the way

The Depression Pilgrim's Journey
The Man Who Walked through Time

we sway from side to side when we trot.
Some of our riders get seasick.

I sway from side to side because of the way my legs work.
Both legs on one side move forward at the same time,
elevating that side.
My "left, right left, right" motion makes my rider feel like
he is in a rocking chair going sideways.

When I was six months old,
special knee pads started to grow on my front legs.
The intelligent Creator knew I had to have them.
They help me lower my 1000 pounds to the ground.

The Depression Pilgrim's Journey
The Man Who Walked through Time

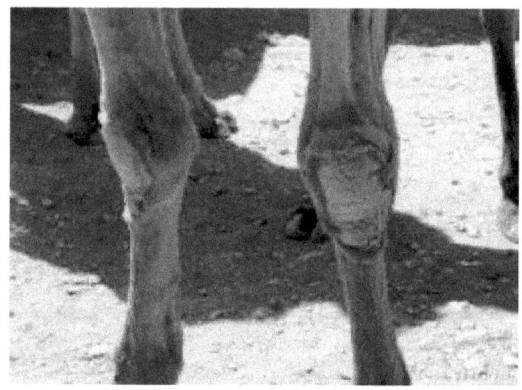

If I didn't have them,

my knees would soon become sore and infected,

and I could never lie down.

I'd die of exhaustion.

By the way,

I don't get thick knee pads because I fall on my knees.

I fall on my knees because I already have these tough pads.

Someone very great thought of me and knew I needed them.

He designed them into my genes.

The Depression Pilgrim's Journey
The Man Who Walked through Time

It's real difficult for me to understand
how some people say I evolved into what I now am.
I'm very technical, highly engineered dromedary camel.
Things like me don't just happen.

They're planned on a drawing board
by Someone very brilliant,
Someone very logical.

John 1:1 says,
"In the beginning was the Word.
And the Word was with God,
and the Word was God."
The Word means "logical, intelligent One."

The Depression Pilgrim's Journey
The Man Who Walked through Time

Reality of the Unseen

"While we look not at the things which are seen but at the things that are not seen;

for the things which are seen are temporal, but the things not seen are eternal" (2 Corinthians 4:18)

I. Mankind recognizes the reality of some things not seen

A. Pain (cannot X-ray it and find; it is subjective)

B. Odor

C. Cold & Heat

D. Darkness (Re: Egyptians "darkness that could be felt" Genesis 21-22)

E. Wind (Jesus to Nicodemus: hear the sound, not see John 3:8)

F. Noise

G. Electricity (substance, or force?)

H. Love

I. Cannot "SEE" any of the above, et al; only the results & effects)

The Depression Pilgrim's Journey
The Man Who Walked through Time

II. Mankind attaches little meaning to some things not seen

A. Thomas: "Except I shall see...I will NOT believe (John 20:25)

B. "Eyes to see and see not..." (Matthew 13:13)

C. "Let their eyes be darkened, that they see not ... " (Psalm 69:23)

D. "Say to the seers, See not, and prophets, Prophesy not" (Isaiah 30:10)

III.   The importance of the unseen

A. Balaam's blindness & his donkey's vision (Numbers 22:21-35)

B. Elisha & his servant Gehazi (2 Kings 6:15-17)

C. "The Angel of the Lord encamps about them that fear...(Psalm 34:7)

D. Daniel saw the vision; those with him saw not (Daniel 10:7)

E. Stephen saw heaven opened ... others saw not (Acts 7:55-59)

F. Peter from prison: wist not that it was true; thought vision (Acts 12:1-16)

The Depression Pilgrim's Journey
The Man Who Walked through Time

G. Paul saw; those with him saw not (Acts 9:1-7)

H. "Hope for that we see not...." (Romans 8:25)

I. "Compassed about with so great a cloud of witnesses" (Hebrews 12:1-ff)

The Depression Pilgrim's Journey
The Man Who Walked through Time

Shipwreck Survivor

The only survivor of a shipwreck washed up on a small, uninhabited island. He prayed feverishly for God to rescue him. Every day, he scanned the horizon for help, but none seemed forthcoming. Exhausted, he eventually managed to build a little shelter out of driftwood to protect himself from the elements and to store his few possessions. One day, after scavenging for food, he arrived home to find his little hut in flames, with smoke rolling up to the sky. He felt the worst had happened, and everything was lost. He was stunned with disbelief, grief, and anger.

He cried out, 'God! How could you do this to me?'

Early the next day, he was awakened by the sound of a ship approaching the island! It had come to rescue him!

'How did you know I was here?' asked the weary man of his rescuers.

'We saw your smoke signal,' they replied.

The Moral of This Story:

It's easy to get discouraged when things are going bad, but we shouldn't lose heart, because God is at work in our lives, even in the midst of our pain and suffering. Remember that the next time your little hut seems to be burning to the ground. It just may be a smoke signal that summons the Grace of God.

The Depression Pilgrim's Journey
The Man Who Walked through Time

Greek Time Kairos vs Chronos

• • • Saturday, September 16, 2006 • E

Having a kairos moment in a chronos world

If you think the headline for this article sounds like Greek, you're right. That language is very definitive and descriptive because the Greeks have several words denoting shades of differences. For example, we use only one word for "love," so we may say, "I love chocolate"; "I love that new suit"; "I love my husband"; "I love God." These have different meanings, but only one word expresses it. The Greeks, on the other hand, have four words for love: storge (family love), eros (sexual love), philia (brotherly love). Philadelphia is called "the city of brotherly love" and has its roots in the Greek word philia and agape (God's love).

The Greeks also have two words for time — chronos, which is ho-hum or watching-the-clock time, and kairos, special time with loved ones, times of inspiration and commitment or God's time. The

Nell Mohney
Inspiration

problem, of course, is that we live so regularly in chronos time that we don't see the kairos moment opportunities all around us.

In his book, "Seizing the Moment," Dr. James Moore invites his readers to look again at the Gospel account of the life of Jesus. In a stress-filled chronos world, Jesus constantly saw opportunities for kairos moments. In a busy street scene, he was the only one to see Zachaeus sitting alone in a sycamore tree. Zachaeus had taken more than his share of taxes he had collected and was, as a result, a lonely and very unpopular man. Jesus went home with the troubled man, and Zachaeus was never the same again.

Or amid the cacophony of sounds in a bustling village square, Jesus heard a blind man and a leper calling for help, and as people crowded around him, he felt the des-

perate touch of a sick woman who in faith touched the hem of his garment. He took time to see these people, bear them and bring hope into the sadness of their worlds. Jesus also took time to enjoy being with his disciples and having dinner and meaningful conversation often in the home of Mary and Martha.

I don't always see the kairos moments staring me in the face, but on a recent Friday night I did. Since our son had just returned from a mission trip to Kenya, Africa, we were eager to see his pictures and hear the details of his journey. He and his wife were coming to our house for dinner along with our granddaughter, Ellen, and her fiance, Ryan Gray. It was great to have them, but my chronos world of deadlines and speaking engagements had left me fatigued and not very sharp as a conversationalist.

Ralph and I were thrilled that Ellen wanted to spend one last night in "her room" at our house before her wed-

ding on Sept. 30. While she transferred some wedding gifts into her parents' car, Ralph and I put the last load of dishes into the dishwasher.

Then in her usual fashion, Ellen bounded up the stairs and called, "Let's talk." Shortly thereafter, she and I were sitting cross-legged in our pajamas on her bed and talking about life and love; about men and marriage; about faith and friends. I became aware that in that kairos moment, I was allowed a glimpse into the soul of a 24-year-old. The moment was so special I almost had to turn my eyes away.

That night, a prayer for myself and for you, the readers, was: "Lord, don't let us stay so bogged down in the business of our chronos world that we miss the kairos moments all around us. Amen."

Nell Mohney is a Christian author, motivational speaker and seminar leader. She may reached at RWMSR18@comcast.net.

The Depression Pilgrim's Journey
The Man Who Walked through Time

Proof of the Human Soul

There is scientific evidence of a living soul that transcends death:

- The year, 1907.
- The place, Haverhill, MA.
- The man, Dr. Duncan MacDougall.

1. NOT a spiritualist.
2. But a man of science.

He set out to disprove the belief in the human soul.

He placed terminally ill patients on delicately balanced scales to determine if there was any change in body weight at the moment of death. There was! Time after time after time, on human beings there was a slight difference in body weight in human beings at the moment of death. And, in no instance, was there any change in the body weight of animals.

He concluded that man, in fact, does have a human soul that escapes the body at the time of death. The human soul weighs between 3/8 ounces and 1½ ounces!

The Depression Pilgrim's Journey
The Man Who Walked through Time

The Soul's Weight (1983)

JUNE 19, 1983

Significa   06-19-1983

By Irving Wallace, David Wallechinsky and Amy Wallace

Annette Kellerman blithely bares all in 1916 film "A Daughter of the Gods".

First Movie Nude

The first star to bare herself in a feature film was Annette Kellerman, in *A Daughter of the Gods* in 1916. A professional swimmer, she'd created a sensation in 1907, when she was arrested for wearing a one-piece swimsuit.

A Daughter of the Gods was planned as an elaborate spectacle. Kellerman was called on to dive from a 100-foot tower, jump into a pool of crocodiles, crash against rocks and tumble down a waterfall. She romped through many of her scenes in the buff.

The film was shot in Jamaica, and no expense was spared. Director Herbert Brenon restored an old Spanish fort, constructed a Moorish city and imported 20 camels for one five-minute scene. Despite all these trappings and Kellerman's nudity, the story was so dull that even its undraped star failed to raise eyebrows.

The real excitement happened off-camera. Unimpressed with Brenon's efforts, studio head William Fox had the film reedited and removed the director's name from the final credits. Fox also barred Brenon from the premiere, but he showed up anyway, disguised behind a set of false whiskers. He reportedly enjoyed the show.

Girls Outsmart Boys

Until 1982, girls in the Swiss canton of Vaud had to earn higher scores than boys to be admitted to high school.

Each year, girls were performing better than boys on the entrance exams, even though they had to learn home arts like sewing, leaving less time for intellectual pursuits. To keep the admittance ratio at 50/50, requirements were set higher for girls.

In June 1981, however, the Swiss passed a constitutional amendment guaranteeing equality of the sexes. This made the Vaud practice illegal, and 12 parents took the issue to court. Conservatives who fought them said, "At the age of high school entrance [11-12], girls have the advantage because they are more mature; more studious, more docile than boys. It is necessary then to rectify the range in favor of the latter."

When the case reached the Swiss Supreme Court, the justices ruled in favor of the girls and equality.

How Much Does Your Soul Weigh? 3/8 — 1½ oz

There is scientific evidence—according to one scientist, at least—that the human soul not only exists but also that the average soul weighs around an ounce.

In 1907, Dr. Duncan MacDougall of Haverhill, Mass., described a series of experiments he'd recently completed at a large hospital. Dr. MacDougall had moved the bed of a dying tuberculosis patient onto a sensitively balanced platform beam scale, then kept close watch on him throughout his final hours. At the precise moment of death, the beam fell and the scale showed a 3/4-ounce weight loss.

Five more terminal patients were similarly weighed over the next 2½ years; at least three also lost weight suddenly at the moment of death—between 3/8 and 1½ ounces. There seemed to be no explanation other than the soul's flight from the body. Just to be certain, MacDougall ran the same experiment on 15 dogs (all lack-

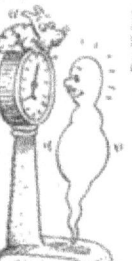

ing souls, according to traditional Judeo-Christian teachings). Not one of the dogs showed any weight loss.

When the doctor published his findings, he emphasized that he was a man of science and not a spiritualist. Yet his experiments, he wrote, appeared to demonstrate scientifically the existence of the soul. Newspapers had a field day with the story, and one proposed that a convicted criminal be weighed as he was being electrocuted to test the doctor's findings. The ghoulish experiment never took place, nor did anyone bother to weigh MacDougall's departing soul when he died

The Depression Pilgrim's Journey
The Man Who Walked through Time

The Laminins Cross in our Bodies

This is a pretty neat story and an interesting thing that few of us know. It's brief, so please read. (FROM A DOCTOR)

A couple of days ago, I was running (I use that term very loosely) on my treadmill, watching a DVD sermon by Louie Giglio... and I was BLOWN AWAY! I want to share what I learned.... He (Louie) was talking about how inconceivably BIG our God is...How He spoke the universe into being. How He breathes stars out of His mouth that are huge, raging balls of fire, etc., etc.

Then he went on to speak of how this star-breathing, universe-creating God ALSO knitted our human bodies together with amazing detail and wonder.

At this point, I am LOVING it (fascinating from a medical standpoint, you know). And I was remembering how I was constantly amazed during medical school as I learned more and more about God's handiwork. I remember so many times thinking, How can ANYONE deny that a Creator did all of this?

Louie went on to talk about how we can trust that the God who created all this, also has the power to hold it all together when things seem to be falling apart...how our loving Creator is also our sustainer. And then I lost my breath. And it wasn't because I was

The Depression Pilgrim's Journey
The Man Who Walked through Time

running my treadmill, either! It was because he started talking about laminin. I knew about laminin.

Here is how Wikipedia describes them: Laminins are a family of proteins that are an integral part of the structural scaffolding of basement membranes in almost every animal tissue. You see, laminins are what hold us together...LITERALLY. They are cell adhesion molecules. They are what hold one cell of our bodies to the next cell. Without them, we would literally fall apart.

And I knew all this already. But what I didn't know is what they LOOKED LIKE.. But now I do. And I have thought about it a thousand times since (already).... Here is what the structure of laminin looks like... AND THIS IS NOT a Christian portrayal of it.... If you look up laminin in any scientific/medical piece of literature, this is what you will see....

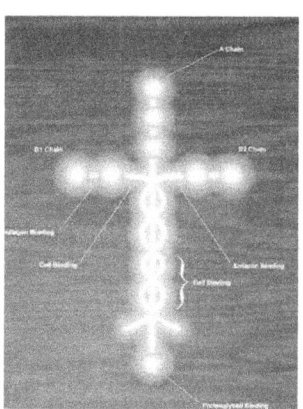

The Depression Pilgrim's Journey
The Man Who Walked through Time

Now tell me that our God is not the coolest!! Amazing. The glue that holds us together… All of us…is in the shape of the cross. Immediately, Colossians 1:15-17 comes to mind. He is the image of the invisible God, the firstborn over all creation. All things were created by Him and for Him. He is before all things, and in him All things hold together. Colossians 1:15-17

Call me crazy. I just think that is very, very, very cool. Thousands of years before the world knew anything about laminin, Paul penned those words. And now we see that from a very literal standpoint, we are held together…..One cell to another…. By the cross.

You would never in a quadrillion years convince me that is anything other than the mark of a Creator who knew exactly what laminin would look like long before Adam breathed his first breath!!

What I found when I googled laminin!!!!!

The Depression Pilgrim's Journey
The Man Who Walked through Time

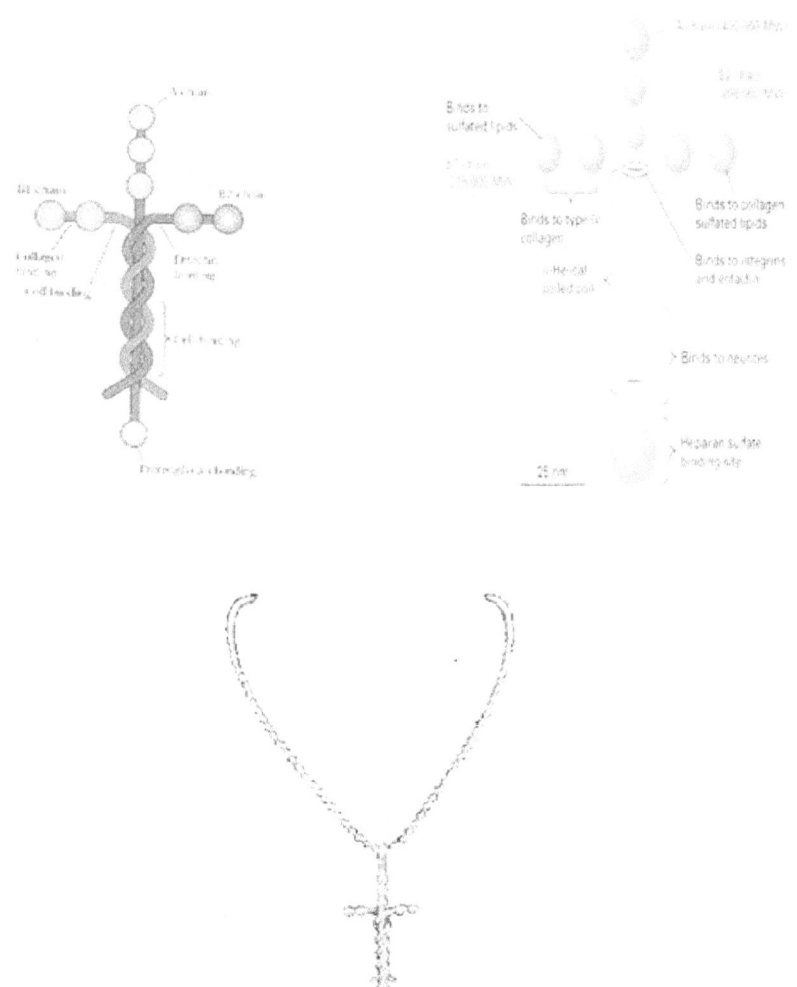

The cross is supposed to be swinging when you receive this. I hope it still is. This is cool – had to pass it on. I think we could all use a miracle. I know I certainly can!

The Depression Pilgrim's Journey
The Man Who Walked through Time

Israel's Order of the Camps

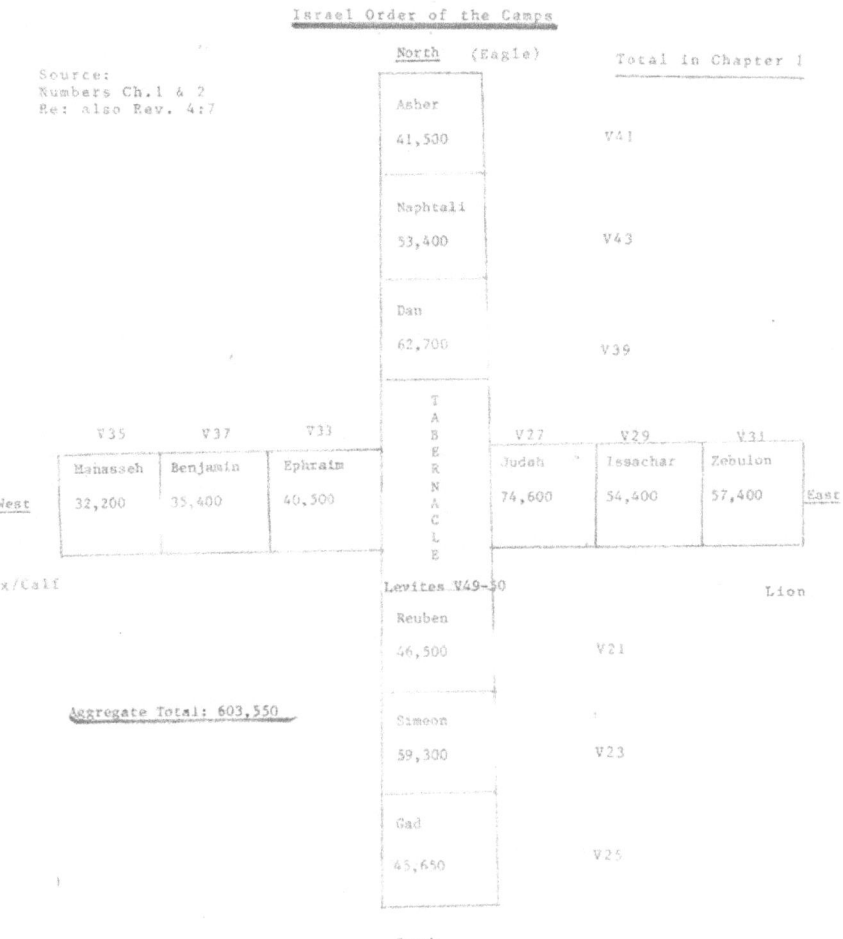

The Depression Pilgrim's Journey
The Man Who Walked through Time

Noah's Ark Lessons

1) Don't miss the boat.

2 Remember, we're all in the same boat.

3) Plan ahead – it wasn't raining when Noah built the ark!

4) Stay fit. When you're 600 years old, you may be asked to do a BIG job.

5) Don't listen to critics. Just get on with the job at hand.

6) Build your future on high ground.

7) For safety's sake, travel in pairs!

8) Speed isn't always an advantage. The snails were on board with the cheetahs!

9) When you're STRESSED out, float a while.

10) Remember the Ark was built by an amateur; the Titanic by professionals!

11) No matter the storm, when you are with God, there's always a rainbow awaiting.

The Depression Pilgrim's Journey
The Man Who Walked through Time

Cohn's Law

"The more time you spend reporting on what you are doing,

The less time you have to do anything.

Stability will be reached when you spend all your time

Doing nothing but reporting on the nothing you are doing."

The Depression Pilgrim's Journey
The Man Who Walked through Time

Murphy's Fundamental Laws

#		#	
1	If Anything Can Go Wrong, Invariably It Will	10	By Making Something Absolutely Clear, Someone Will Become Confused
2	Nothing Is Ever As Simple As It First Seems	11	Every Clarification Breeds New Questions
3	Everything You Decide To Do Costs More Than First Estimated	12	You Can Fool Some Of The People All Of The Time And All Of The People Some Of The Time And That Is Sufficient
4	Every Activity Takes More Time Than You Have	13	Persons Disagreeing With Your Facts Are Always Emotional And Employ Faulty Reasoning
5	By Trying To Please Everybody, Somebody Will Be Displeased	14	Enough Research Will Tend To Support Your Conclusions
6	It Is A Fundamental Law Of Nature That Nothing Ever Quite Works Out	15	The Greater The Importance Of Decisions To Be Made The Larger Must Be The Committee Assigned To Make Them
7	It Is Easier To Make A Commitment Or To Get Involved In Something Than To Get Out Of It	16	The More Urgent The Need For Decision The Less Apparent Becomes The Identity Of The Decision-maker
8	Whatever You Set Out To Do, Something Else Must Be Done First	17	The More Complex The Idea Or Technology The More Simple-Minded Is The Opposition
9	If You Improve Or Tinker With Something Long Enough, Eventually It Will Break Or Misfunction	18	Each Profession Talks To Itself In Its Own Unique Language. Apparently There Is No Rosetta Stone.

Compliments: Paul A. Ritch 2019

The Depression Pilgrim's Journey
The Man Who Walked through Time

Murphy's Addends, or 'The Gospel according to Ritch'

- No matter how many sox you put in the washer, there's always 1 less that comes out!
- You pay off the mortgage on the auto, then within days it has a 'bolt-hemorrhage' in the highway!
- You finally pay off the mortgage on the house, the roof starts leaking, the foundation crumbles, and you didn't renew the insurance when you burned the mortgage!
- You fly non-stop: Atlanta-to-LA, luggage winds up in Houston!
- You wait in line 1 hour at the bank, then the teller closes just as you get to the window!
- You use the drive-in window next time, and the vacuum tube conveyor dies with your endorsed check mid-stream!
- Just when you learn all the answers, the questions change!
- You make copies of your resume on the office copier, and it breaks down while you're standing there!
- Upward mobility gives you a choice spot in suburbia, then next week they build a massive shopping center next door!
- You finally get that long-awaited promotion to management, then next week they cut corporate expenses

The Depression Pilgrim's Journey
The Man Who Walked through Time

by starting with management ... LIFO method (Last-in-first-out)!

- You call home to advise the wife that you will be late for dinner, and she's already left a note that dinner is in the 'fridge'!

- You finally join the 'sexual revolution', only to find out that you are out of ammunition!

- You wake up one morning a couple of decades later to find out that those salt pills they fed you in military boot camp, finally started working!

- You kill your obstinate teenager, and find that they won't let you call it 'delayed abortion!'

- You have a wife, a girlfriend, and a note at the bank, and they all are 'overdue' at the same time!

The Depression Pilgrim's Journey
The Man Who Walked through Time

Born Before 1945

To all of us born before 1945 ... WE ARE SURVIVORS!! Consider the changes we have witnessed. We were born before television; before penicillin; before polio shots, frozen food, Xerox, plastic, contact lenses, frisbees, and 'THE PILL'.

We were born before radar, credit cards, split atoms, laser beams, and ballpoint pens; before pantyhose, dishwashers, clothes dryers, electric blankets, air conditioners, drip-dry clothes; ... and, before man walked on the moon.

We got married first and then lived together. How quaint can you be?

In our time, closets were for clothes, not for 'coming out of'. 'Bunnies' were small rabbits, and rabbits were not Volkswagons! Designer Jeans were scheming girls named Jean or Jeanne, and having a 'meaningful relationship' meant getting along well with our cousins.

We thought 'fast food' was what catholics ate during Lent, and 'Outer Space' was the back of the local movie house.

We were born before 'house-husbands', 'gay rights', 'computer-dating', 'dual-careers', and 'commuter marriages'. We were before day-care centers, group therapy, and nursing homes. We never heard of FM radio, tape-decks, electric typewriters, artificial hearts,

The Depression Pilgrim's Journey
The Man Who Walked through Time

word-processors, yogurt, and guys wearing earrings! For us, 'time-sharing' meant togetherness, not computers or condominiums; and a 'chip' meant a piece of wood; 'hardware' meant hardware, and 'software' was not even a word!

In 1940, 'Made-in-Japan' meant 'junk'; and the term 'making-out' referred to how well you did on exams. Pizzas, McDonald's, and instant coffee were unheard of.

We hit the scene when there were 5 & 10 cent stores, where you bought things for five and ten cents! The local pharmacy sold ice cream cones for a nickel or a dime. For one nickel, you could ride a streetcar, make a phone call, buy a cola, or enough postage stamps to mail one letter and two postal cards. You could buy a new Chevy coupe for $600, but who could afford one? And a pity too, for gasoline was 11 cents a gallon!

In our day, cigarette smoking was fashionable; 'GRASS' was mowed; 'COKE' was a cold drink; and 'POT' was something for cooking! 'ROCK MUSIC' was a grandma's lullaby, and 'AIDS' were helpers in the school principal's office.

We were certainly not before the difference in the sexes was 'discovered', but were before the sex-change. And we were the last generation so dumb as to think you needed a husband to have a

The Depression Pilgrim's Journey
The Man Who Walked through Time

baby. No wonder we are confused. BUT WE SURVIVED! And, we're still holding our own in the crazy 'eighties'!!!

The Depression Pilgrim's Journey
The Man Who Walked through Time

Excuses vs. Commitment
II Timothy 2:2; II Timothy 4:1-ff

A state of being obligated or emotionally impelled. To be put in charge or trust. Pledged.

To perform; to practice; exercise; be busy with. To mimic the Energizer Bunny. Stay the course. Some fear failure. To guarantee not failing, NEVER TRY!

Re: Bacon & eggs. The chicken made a contribution. The Pig gave his all!

THESE individuals are said to have FAILED (sometimes, often) before they succeeded:

A. Engineer who did not design a reverse gear in his first auto (Henry Ford)

B. Rejected by Decca Records because 'guitars were on the way out' (Beatles)

C. Illustrator told by his Editor to pursue another line of work (Walt Disney)

D. Skinny kid who hated his looks and was beaten up by bullies (Charles Atlas)

E. Ill, in debt, and depressed, wrote 'The Messiah' in a few hours (Handel)

The Depression Pilgrim's Journey
The Man Who Walked through Time

F. Obese, bald, deformed eccentric who became a reclusive thinker (Socrates)

G. Conductor/composer's greatest works after becoming deaf (Beethoven)

H. Deaf/blind @ 18 months; became a great writer/philanthropist (Helen Keller)

I. Lost first 7 attempts at public office, and other failures (Abraham Lincoln)

SUPPOSE, in the face of adversity, these had quit??

A. Joshua & Caleb had joined the unbelievers (grasshoppers)? (Num. 13:33)

B. The Israelites had wearied & aborted the trips around Jericho? (Joshua 6:5)

C. Gideon's 300 had quit in the face of astronomical odds? (Judges 7:19)

D. David had decided on SIZE alone? Goliath would have lived. (1Samuel 7)

E. Jews had listened to Sanballet & Tobia @ the wall (Nehemiah 4:1-3)

F. Jesus had quit in Gethsemane when blood as drops of blood? (Mt. 26:3

The Depression Pilgrim's Journey
The Man Who Walked through Time

THESE Used What They Had (God does not call the qualified; He qualifies the 'called')

Re: I Corinthians 1:26

1. MOSES had a rod; it became a wand (Exodus 4:2).

2. DAVID had a sling; with it he slew a giant (I Samuel 17:49).

3. A Jewish maiden had only a voice; she told Naaman of Elisha (2 Kgs 5:1-14).

4. A LAD had 5 loaves, 2 fish; with it, Jesus fed @ 5,000 (John 6:1-13).

5. A widow had only two mites; millions were inspired by her giving (Mk. 12:42-44).

6. Dorcas had only a sewing kit; she helped the poor (Acts 9:36-39).

WHAT is in your hand? It all depends on whose hands it is in!

1. A basketball in my hands is worth about $19; in Michael Jordan's $33 million.

2. A baseball in my hands is worth about $5; in Roger Clemons @ $475 million.

The Depression Pilgrim's Journey
The Man Who Walked through Time

3. A rod in my hand will ward off an angry dog; in Moses' hands: part the sea.

4. A slingshot in my hands: a kid's toy; in David's hands, a giant slayer.

5. Five loaves & two fish in my hands: a sandwich. In Jesus' a meal for 4,000.

6. Nails in my hand, a birdhouse; in Jesus' salvation for the whole world.

ABRAM was 75 (Gen.12)

MOSES was 80 (Ex. 7:7)

JOSHUA was 80+ (Josh. 13:1)

CALEB was 85 (Jos. 14)

DANIEL in 90's

PAUL "the 'aged" (Phil. 9)

JOHN in 90's (on Patmos).

The next time you feel like God cannot use you, REMEMBER these:

A. Noah was a drunk (off the ark, planted a vineyard, made wine Gen. 9:20-21)

The Depression Pilgrim's Journey
The Man Who Walked through Time

 B. Abraham was too old (75, Gen. 12:4), and was a liar (Gen. 12:9-20)

 C. Jacob was a liar (Gen. 27:19)

 D. Leah was ugly (Gen. 29:17)

 E. Joseph (OT) was abused as a child (Gen. 37:14-28)

 F. Moses had a speech impediment (Ex. 4:10-14; Ex. 6:12)

 G. Gideon was afraid (Judges 6:27)

 H. Samson was a womanizer (terminal 'skirt-itis' … Judges 14:7; 16:10)

 I. Rahab was a harlot (Joshua 2:1)

 J. Jeremiah was too young ('a child' Jer.1:7)

 K. David was an adulterer and a murderer (II Sam. 11:4-15)

 L. Elijah was suicidal (under the juniper tree, fleeing Jezebel, I Kings 19:4)

 M. Isaiah preached naked & barefoot 3 years (Isaiah 20:2-3)

 N. Jonah ran from God as an unwilling missionary (Jonah 1:3)

 O. Naomi lost her husband and both sons (Ruth 1: 3-5)

The Depression Pilgrim's Journey
The Man Who Walked through Time

P. Job went bankrupt (lost oxen, asses, camels, sheep, children Job 1:9-21)

Q. John the Baptist ate bugs (locusts & wild honey Mt. 3:1-4)

R. Simon Peter denied Jesus (speech betrayed, so he cursed/denied Mt. 26:73-74)

S. Thomas doubted Him (John 20:25)

T. The Disciples fell asleep while praying (Mk. 14:32-37; Luke 22:39-45)

U. Lazarus' sister, Martha, worried about everything (Luke 10:40-42)

V. Mary Magdalene had been devil-possessed (Mk. 16:9; Luke 8:2)

W. The Samaritan woman was divorced five (5) times! (John 4:7-18)

X. Zacchaeus was too small (Luke 19:2-5)

Y. Paul was too religious (Acts 7:58 through 8:3)

Z. Timothy was too young (I Tim. 4:12) & had ulcers (1 Tim. 5:23)

AA. And, Lazarus was DEAD!!! (John 11:14)

The Depression Pilgrim's Journey
The Man Who Walked through Time

But God used all these unlikely vessels to His glory! (Re: 1 Corinthians 1:26-27).

Quit looking for 'excuses'!

Be COMMITED! GO OUT AND DO SOMETHING!

Borrowed and "En-Ritched"

The Depression Pilgrim's Journey
The Man Who Walked through Time

End of Chapter

Appendix A: About the Author
Paul A. Ritch Education, Experience, Honors, Etc.
Education:

- Graduate Cedartown (GA) High School; Sr. Valedictorian; Jr. Class President.

- Studied Theology and Business at Shorter College, Rome, GA.

- Graduate US Army "Series-10" Pre-Commission Program (Ft. Benning, GA).

- Graduate US Army "Communications Officers School" (Ft. Knox, KY).

- Graduate Southern Technical Institute "Engineering Illustrations" Program.

- Baccalaureate(x3); Valedictorian; Chaplain; Sr. Class President; Tennessee Temple.

- Bachelor of Bible equivalency; Tennessee Temple.

- Graduate of Theology Degree; Valedictorian; Chaplain; Tennessee Temple.

- Master of Divinity equivalency; Trinity Bible Seminary.

- Master's Degree Summa Cum Laude; University of Chattanooga, TN

The Depression Pilgrim's Journey
The Man Who Walked through Time

- Doctoral Degree Highest Honors; University of Tennessee at Knoxville.

- Graduate National Management Association's (NMA) Management Program

- Graduate Medical Management Practice Institute (MMPI)

- Et.al.

Experience:

- Farmer, soldier, pastor (GA & AL), evangelist, computer pioneer, educator, manager, professional.

- After pastorate, evangelist, served in academia as professor/administrator; helped

pioneer technical education & Community College system of TN

- College Administrator & Professor of Computer Science, Psychology, Business, and Management.

- Manager of Major Systems, Tennessee Valley Authority (TVA), including IPDS System

(Cresap/McCormick/Pagett, Chicago) and MAMS Project (Arthur Anderson & Co.)

- Law Firm Administrator at Partner Level, Chambliss, Bahner, and others

- Consultant to government, industry, education, and the professions.

The Depression Pilgrim's Journey
The Man Who Walked through Time

- Christian counselor to untold myriads of hurting hearts.
- Volunteer minister to the elderly and dying in the FPCC and Chattanooga region.
- FPCC Hospital Visitation Coordinator; FPCC Pulpit Committee 2008-2009.
- Filled pulpits in area churches across many denominations.
- For more than six decades, evangelized, married the living, and buried the dead.

Honors and Awards

- High School Junior Class President 1952
- High School Senior Class Valedictorian 1953
- National Beta Club 1952, 1953
- High School Senior Class "Who's Who" (Most Intellectual) 1953
- Daughters of the American Revolution (DAR) "Good Citizenship Award" 1953
- Teenage speaker on local WGAA-1340 Radio … sponsored by area Churches
- Young Adult speaker on WROM-TV (Now WTVC-9 Chattanooga, TN)
- Pastor Salem Baptist Church, Pisgah, AL

The Depression Pilgrim's Journey
The Man Who Walked through Time

- Pastor Temple Baptist Church, Marietta, GA
- Pastor Mount Olive Baptist Church, Rossville, GA
- Evangelist (until retirement to care for dying spouse)
- College Senior Class President and Valedictorian 1963
- University Chaplain: Combined Colleges, Bible School, Seminary 1963
- D. B. Eastep Memorial Award for Outstanding Christian Service 1963
- President College Alumni Honor Society 1963 and 1964
- Developed the world's 1st "custom programmed" Carpet Industry computer system. IBM reps brought curious business men from Europe to see it in person!
- Recruited as a member of the founding faculty, Chattanooga State Technical Institute

  (CSTI) Later renamed Chattanooga State Technical Community College (CSTCC)
- Helped pioneer technical education for the State of Tennessee at CSTI
- Helped develop the world's first academic program in Computer Science

  Accredited by the Engineers' Council for Professional Development (ECPD)

The Depression Pilgrim's Journey
The Man Who Walked through Time

- Established CSTI as the official test site for the "Certified Data Processor" (CDP) exam

- Helped Dr. Dean Banta develop curriculum for the first TN community college system

- CSTCC Articulating Rep to the State University & Community College System of TN

- CSTCC Articulating Rep to the Land-Grant University of Tennessee System

- CSTCC Articulating Rep to the Tennessee Higher Education Council (THEC)

- Architect and Head of Chattanooga State's original Computing Center in 1967 and later designated as the "Dr. Paul A Ritch Data Center."

- Worked with the Educational Testing Service on the CLEP program

- "Who's Who in the Computer Field" 1968-69

- "Who's Who in Computers and Data Processing" 1969-1974

- "Who's Who in Computer Education and Research" 1973-76

- "Who's Who in the South and Southwest" 14th 1974 and 15th 1975

The Depression Pilgrim's Journey
The Man Who Walked through Time

- "Dictionary of International Biography" Vol. IX 1972-73; Vol. XII 1975-76
- "Who's Who in America" 39th edition
- President, CSTI Administrative-Staff Council 1971-72
- President Tennessee Technical Educational Council (TTEC)
- Vice President, Tennessee Vocational Association (TVA)
- Outstanding Educator of America 1974 and again 1975
- Freedom Award by Freedoms Foundation at Valley Forge 1972
- President Highland SERTOMA Club 1973-1974
- Board Chairman Highland SERTOMA Club 1974-75
- "SERTOMAN-of-the-Year" Highland Club; Chattanooga TN, 1972-73
- SERTOMA International "Centurion" Award 1972-73
- SERTOMA International "Tribune" Award 1973-74
- SERTOMA International "Senator" Award 1974-75
- International Data Processing Management Association's "Computer Sciences Man-of-the-Year" 1973-1974 and again 1974-1975

The Depression Pilgrim's Journey
The Man Who Walked through Time

Chattanooga Chapter and USA Region-7 (TN, AL, GA, FL, SC)

- Manager of Major Systems, Tennessee Valley Authority (TVA) 1976-81

- "International Men of Achievement," Cambridge, England, 1975 & again 1976

- "Community Leaders and Noteworthy Americans" 10th edition 1978

- "International Who's Who of Intellectuals" Vol. I 1978

- "Directory of Distinguished Americans" 1981

- "International Register of Profiles" 6th edition 1982

- Consultant to government, industry, education, and the professions, 1983.

Over one hundred fifty clients across the American landscape are using leading-edge state-of-the-art technology and ergonomic allocation of scarce resources for synergistic profitability, efficiencies, and enhanced human satisfaction.

- Member TN Private Investigation & Polygraph Commission, two terms, 2006-2017

Appointed by one Democrat Governor and one Republican Governor; never met either

- Regularly conducted area worship services, weddings, and funerals
- Filled in for Cornerstone Presbyterian (2007-2009) while they sought a Pastor
- Filled in for Silverdale Cumberland (2009-2010) while they sought a Pastor
- Filled in regularly at South Seminole Baptist (TN) in the Pastor's absence
- Keynote speaker for a number of national conventions, including the IAA annual meeting, co-keynote with J. Presper Eckert (co-architect of the world's first computer at the University of PA, 1946), and USAF Technical Director

Professional and Related Associations

- American Association of University Professors (AAUP) 1968-1970
- Association of Educational Data Systems (AEDS) 1969-1971
- Society of Data Educators (SDE), 1971-73
- Data Processing Management Association (DPMA) 1964-1977

    (Treasurer 1968-1970)

- American Vocational Association (AVA) 1966-1977

The Depression Pilgrim's Journey
The Man Who Walked through Time

- Tennessee Vocational Association (TVA) 1966-1977

    (Vice-President 1974-1976)

- Tennessee Technical Education Council (TTEC) 1969-1977

- (President 1974-1976)

- SERTOMA 1970-1977 Chairman 1974-1975, President 1973-1974,

    Vice-President 1972-1973

- International Platform Association (IPA) 1975-1978

- Phi Delta Kappa (PDK) 1973-1983

- National Management Association (NMA) 1976-1983

- Association of Computing Machinery (ACM) 1976-1983

- National Retired Teachers Association (NRTA) 1976-1983

- American Bar Association (ABA) 1982-1983

- Association of Legal Administrators (ALA) 1982-1983

The Depression Pilgrim's Journey
The Man Who Walked through Time

Paul A. Ritch Representative Clients

GOVERNMENT

    General Services Administration; Washington, DC

    National Bureau of Standards; Washington, DC

    Tennessee Valley Authority; Knox/Chatta, TN & Muscle Shoals, AL

    Hamilton County Health Department; Chattanooga, TN

EDUCATION

    State University and Community College System of Tennessee

    Chattanooga State Technical Institute; Chattanooga, TN

    Dalton Junior College; Dalton, GA

    Cleveland State Community College; Cleveland, TN

    Truett-McConnell College; Cleveland, GA

    University of Tennessee, Knoxville, TN, Chattanooga, TN

INDUSTRY

    Modern Carpet Industries; Dalton, GA

    Star Finishing Company; Dalton, GA

    Coronet Carpet Industries; Dalton, GA

    World Carpet, Inc., Dalton, GA

    Cabin Crafts, Inc., Dalton, GA

The Depression Pilgrim's Journey
The Man Who Walked through Time

Redfield Carpet Company; Dalton, GA

Magic Chef, Inc., Cleveland, TN

Cherokee Area Council, Boy Scouts of America

Tennessee Optometry Association (C. Wayne Shearer, Pres.)

Metropolitan Council for Community Services; Chattanooga, TN

Data Processing Management Association; Chattanooga, TN

Educational Testing Service; Princeton, NJ

Tennessee Vocational Association; Nashville, TN

Morgan Manufacturing Company; Etowah, TN

WhiteCrest Carpet Mills, Inc., Dalton, GA

Trenton Telephone Company, Inc.; Trenton, GA

Trenton Water Company; Trenton, GA

Ringgold Telephone Company, Inc., Ringgold, GA

Seco Manufacturing Company; Cleveland, TN

General Electric Company; Rome, GA

Cumberland Mills, Inc., Chatsworth, GA

M & M Carpets; Dalton, GA

Vol State Chemical; Chattanooga, TN

**The Depression Pilgrim's Journey
The Man Who Walked through Time**

Circle C Federal Credit Union; Chattanooga, TN

Cooke Manufacturing Company, Inc., Cleveland, TN

Camera & Craft; East Ridge, TN

Bradley Block Company; Cleveland, TN

Davis Diggers; Cleveland, TN

TAG Construction Company; Cleveland, TN

Marsh-Tennessee Company; Chattanooga, TN

Marsh Specialty Packaging; Chattanooga, TN

Robinson Building Center, Inc., Cleveland, TN

Dayton Concrete; Dayton, TN

Venture Screen Printing; Chattanooga, TN

American Capital; Chattanooga, TN

Herron's Gilman Paint; Cleveland, TN

Prism Data Systems; Indianapolis, IN

North Georgia Credit Bureau; Lafayette, GA

Allstate Credit Services (Collections); Rossville, GA

Hamilton Collections; East Ridge, TN

Northwest Georgia Collection Agency; Ft. Oglethorpe, GA

Daleco Adjustment Services; Chattanooga & East Ridge, TN

Federal Exchange & Recovery; Chattanooga, TN

The Depression Pilgrim's Journey
The Man Who Walked through Time

Federal Equity Corporation; Chattanooga, TN

Walls Newspapers (56 US cities); Austin, TX/Birmingham, AL

Cleveland Daily Banner; Cleveland, TN

Herald Citizen; Cookeville, TN

Daily Mountain Eagle; Jasper, AL

St. John Valley Times; Madawaska, ME

Abilene Reflector-Chronicle; Abilene, KS

Cartersville Daily; Cartersville, GA

A&O Air; Chattanooga, TN

Comfort by Design, Inc.; Chattanooga, TN

LEGAL

Chambliss/Bahner/Crutchfield/Gaston/Irwin; Chattanooga, TN

Attorney William Slack; LaFayette, GA

MEDICAL

Drs. Jones, Dickinson, and Ramsey; Hixson, TN

Arthritis Associates; Chattanooga, TN

Children's Diagnostic Center; Chattanooga, TN

Drs. Boatwright/Miller/Mills; Hixson, TN

Northgate Medical Center; Hixson, TN

The Depression Pilgrim's Journey
The Man Who Walked through Time

Plaza Orthopedics, PC; Chattanooga, TN

Dr. Lester Littell III; Chattanooga, TN

Cleveland Eye Clinic; Cleveland, TN

Orthopedic Therapy Center of Chattanooga, TN

Dr. Clay Pickard; Chattanooga, TN

Drs. Miller/Mills/Abell/Bolton; Hixson, TN

Beacon Health Alliance; Chattanooga, TN

Osteoscan, Inc.; Chattanooga, TN

Dr. Dennis Stohler; Chattanooga, TN

Dr. Thomas M. Beahm; Chattanooga, TN

RELIGIOUS

Baptist International Missions; Chattanooga, TN

Changed Lives TV & Radio Ministry; Chattanooga, TN

Miscellaneous

Others too legion to enumerate

Appendix B: Poems

Then

Beyond this haze of human hurt

On some Elysian plain I'll dwell;

Where wars will wane, and crime shall cease,

And life shall no more fail.

'Tomorrow' there shall never come

For day shall never end;

Unceasing songs of Saints now home

Will waft o'er there as voices blend

No night there'll be, but twilight's hour

Shall chase away the gloom;

No crepe there'll cling on those fair doors,

No shroud of death will mar our room

Death's sting shall then have been plucked out

Its fear removed by love more grown;

Corrupt shall change with celestial shout,

And the grave shall gasp its final groan!

Unloosed from time whose hands now hold

With freedom's air we shall explore;

World on world as yet untold,

And never viewed by man before

Dr Paul A Ritch

The Depression Pilgrim's Journey
The Man Who Walked through Time

A Tree

With apologies to Joyce Kilmer

A tree calls out to a passing world,
"Why haste you by in such a whirl?
Know you not that all too fast
Your race is o'er, your time is past?
So, stop a while and think with me,
Although I'm only a lowly tree,
A lesson I have to share with you,
Which, if you'll learn, you'll think anew.
Though I've not moved from this same spot
Since but a seed cast on this plot,
So much I've learned and more I've seen
Than many of you through effort keen.
Mere chance it seems that here I grew,
Yet birds found rest as here they flew.
My shade was playground for many a child;
And, once I served as a 'landmark', filed.
Although I've never ventured out
Into yon world and roamed about,
A special place, I believe I fill

The Depression Pilgrim's Journey
The Man Who Walked through Time

By being here and standing still.
For, standing still, when He speaks, I hear;
And speak He does year after year.
He speaks in the wind that stirs my leaves,
Whether a raging storm or a summer breeze.
He speaks in the laughter of young here playing
And by yon horses in the meadow neighing.
He speaks by the lovers whose names appear
Upon my trunk, both front and rear.
He speaks in the sounds of nature's calling,
And by my leaves as they are falling.
He speaks in the little birds here nesting
And also in those who are only resting.
So, you see, without one hurry
I'm bountifully blessed without one worry.
I've seen it all that is finally worthwhile,
And never traveled, not even a mile.
I've simply stood still and carefully listened
Even in winter, as here snow glistened.
Each day my branches uplift, I hold,
As reaching for Him who gave them mold.

The Depression Pilgrim's Journey
The Man Who Walked through Time

In humble submission to His ordaining,

I've shared by giving ... yet, much more gaining!"

© 10-25-1965 Paul A. Ritch, BA(x3), BB, ThG, MDiv. (Equi), MEd, PhD(x2), CDP, CDE, CCP, CM, LPI

The Depression Pilgrim's Journey
The Man Who Walked through Time

I Met God

by Ralph Cushman

I met God in the morning,

when my day was at its best.

And His Presence came like sunrise,

like a glory in my breast.

All day long His Presence lingered,

all day long, He stayed with me.

And we sailed in perfect calmness,

O'er a very troubled sea.

Other ships were blown and battered;

Other ships were sore distressed.

But the winds that seemed to drive them,

Brought to us such peace and rest.

Then I thought of other mornings,

With a keen remorse of mind,

When I too had loosed the moorings,

with the Savior left behind.

So I think I know the secret,

learned from many a troubled way;

You must seek God in the morning

if you want Him through the day.

The Depression Pilgrim's Journey
The Man Who Walked through Time

I've Dreamed Many Dreams

I've dreamed many dreams that never came true.
I've seen them vanish at dawn.
But I've realized enough of my dreams, thank God
To make me want to dream on.

I've prayed many prayers when no answer came,
Though I waited patient and long.
But, answers have come to enough of my prayers,
To make me keep praying on

I've trusted many a friend that failed,
And left me to weep alone.
But, I've found enough of my friends true blue,
To make me keep trusting on.

I've sown many seeds that fell by the way,
For the birds to feed upon.
But I've held enough golden sheaves in my hand,
To make me keep sowing on.

I've drained the cup of disappointment and pain,
And gone many days without song.
But, I've sipped enough nectar from the Roses of life

The Depression Pilgrim's Journey
The Man Who Walked through Time

To make me want to live on.

By Ron DeMarco

Borrowed and "En-Ritched"

Paul A. Ritch, BA(x3), BB, ThG, MDiv (equiv), MEd, PhD(x2), CDP, CDE, CCP, CM, LPI

The Depression Pilgrim's Journey
The Man Who Walked through Time

A Builder

A builder built a temple,
He wrought it with grace and skill.
Pillars and groins and arches,
All fashioned to work his will.

Men said as they say it's beauty
"It shall never know decay.
Great is thy skill, o builder!
Thy fame shall endure for aye."

A teacher built a temple,
With loving and infinite care,
Planning each arch with patience,
Laying each stone with prayer.

None praised her unceasing efforts,
None knew of her wondrous plan.
For the temple the teacher built,
Was unseen by the eyes of man.

The Depression Pilgrim's Journey
The Man Who Walked through Time

Gone is the builder's temple,

Crumbled into dust.

Low lies each stately pillar,

Food for consuming rust.

But the temple the teacher built,

Will last while the ages roll.

For the temple the teacher built,

Was a child's immortal soul!

Author unknown

Borrowed and "En-Ritched"

Paul A. Ritch

The Depression Pilgrim's Journey
The Man Who Walked through Time

At My Mother's Knee

I have worshipped in churches and chapels, I have prayed in the busy street;

I have sought my God and found Him, where the waves of the ocean beat.

I have knelt in the silent forest, in the shade of some ancient tree,

But the dearest of all my altars was raised at my mother's knee.

I have listened to God in His temple, I have caught His voice in the crowd;

I have heard Him speak when the breakers were booming long and loud;

When the winds play soft in the treetops, my Father has talked to me;

But I never have heard Him more clearly than I did at my mother's knee.

The things in my life that are worthy were born in my mother's breast;

And breathed into mine by the magic of the love her life expressed.

The Depression Pilgrim's Journey
The Man Who Walked through Time

The years that have brought me to manhood have taken her far from me;

But memory keeps me from straying too far from my mother's knee.

God, make me the man of her vision, and purge me of all selfishness!

God, keep me true to her standards, and help me to live to bless!

God, hallow the holy impress of the day that used to be,

And keep me a pilgrim forever, to the shrine at my mother's knee.

Anonymous

Borrowed & "En-Ritched" by Paul A. Ritch 12-26-1985

The Depression Pilgrim's Journey
The Man Who Walked through Time

I Miss You

A million times I've needed you,

A million times I've cried.

If love alone could have saved you,

You never would have died.

In life, I loved you dearly,

In death, I love you still.

For in my heart you have a place,

No one else can ever fill.

It broke my heart to see you go,

But you did not go alone.

For part of me went with you,

The day God took you home.

Borrowed From: Natacha Janssens (Facebook)

"En-Ritched" by Paul A. Ritch BA(x3), BB, ThG, MDiv (equiv), MEd, PhD(x2), CDP, CDE, CCP, CM, LPI

The Depression Pilgrim's Journey
The Man Who Walked through Time

If

By Rudyard Kipling

If you can keep your head when all about you

Are losing theirs and blaming it on you;

If you can trust yourself when all men doubt you,

But make allowance for their doubting too;

If you can wait and not be tired by waiting,

Or, being lied about, don't deal in lies,

Or, being hated, don't give way to hating,

And yet don't look too good, nor talk too wise;

If you can dream - and not make dreams your master;

If you can think - and not make thoughts your aim;

If you can meet with triumph and disaster

And treat those two impostors just the same;

If you can bear to hear the truth you've spoken

Twisted by knaves to make a trap for fools,

Or watch the things you gave your life to broken,

And stoop and build 'em up with worn-out tools;

The Depression Pilgrim's Journey
The Man Who Walked through Time

If you can make one heap of all your winnings

And risk it on one turn of pitch-and-toss,

And lose, and start again at your beginnings

And never breathe a word about your loss;

If you can force your heart and nerve and sinew

To serve your turn long after they are gone,

And so hold on when there is nothing in you

Except the will which says to them: "Hold on";

If you can talk with crowds and keep your virtue,

Or walk with kings - nor lose the common touch;

If neither foes nor loving friends can hurt you;

If all men count with you, but none too much;

If you can fill the unforgiving minute

With sixty seconds' worth of distance run -

Yours is the Earth and everything that's in it,

And - which is more - you'll be a Man, my son!

The Depression Pilgrim's Journey
The Man Who Walked through Time

Appendix C: Selected works of Art by Joyce

Joyce Ann Price at age 16

Joyce Ann Ritch at age 44

The Depression Pilgrim's Journey
The Man Who Walked through Time

Joyce Ann Ritch at age 48

Joyce Ann Ritch at age 72

The Depression Pilgrim's Journey
The Man Who Walked through Time

Joyce Ann Ritch at age 74

Joyce Memorial 2018

The Depression Pilgrim's Journey
The Man Who Walked through Time

Joyce 1975 Tiger

Joyce 1979 the cardinal issue

The Depression Pilgrim's Journey
The Man Who Walked through Time

Joyce 1975 Virgin Wool

Joyce 1978 Waterfall

Joyce 1981 Non Obj1 High Museum

The Depression Pilgrim's Journey
The Man Who Walked through Time

What Will Matter

By Michael Josephson

Ready or not, someday it will all come to an end.

There will be no more sunrises, no minutes, hours, or days.

All the things you collected, whether treasured or forgotten, will pass to someone else

Your wealth, fame, and temporal power will shrivel to irrelevance.

It will not matter what you owned or what you were owed.

Your grudges, resentments, frustrations, and jealousies will finally disappear.

So too, your hopes, ambitions, plans, and to-do lists will expire.

The wins and losses that once seemed so important will fade away.

It won't matter where you came from

or what side of the tracks you lived on at the end.

It won't matter whether you were beautiful or brilliant.

Even your gender and skin color will be irrelevant.

So, what will matter?

How will the value of your days be measured?

What will matter is not what you bought

but what you built, not what you got but what you gave.

What will matter is not your success

The Depression Pilgrim's Journey
The Man Who Walked through Time

    but your significance.

What will matter is not what you learned

    but what you taught.

What will matter is every act of integrity,

    compassion, courage, or sacrifice

      that enriched, empowered, or encouraged others

    to emulate your example.

What will matter is not your competence

    but your character.

What will matter is not how many people you knew,

    but how many will feel a lasting loss when you're gone.

What will matter is not your memories

    but the memories that live in those who loved you.

is how long you will be remembered,

    by whom, and for what.

Living a life that matters doesn't happen by accident.

    It's not a matter of circumstance but of choice.

Choose to live a life that matters.

The Depression Pilgrim's Journey
The Man Who Walked through Time

Paul Ritch link to YouTube:

For PC/Laptop: https://www.YouTube.com/@paulritch3244

Click "Videos" under picture, then choose which to view.

For Cellphone: YouTube.com/@paulritch3244

Click on Picture, "Videos" under picture, choose which to view.

www.ingramcontent.com/pod-product-compliance
Lightning Source LLC
Chambersburg PA
CBHW050726010526
44107CB00009B/751